Presented to:

Joseph E. Williams, III

By:

Terry + Joyce Moore

Date:

_6-17-02_

MY PERSONAL PROMISE BIBLE FOR GRADUATES

Honor Books
Tulsa, Oklahoma

My Personal Promise Bible for Graduates
ISBN 1-56292-389-7
45-253-00259
Copyright © 2002 by Honor Books
P.O. Box 55388
Tulsa, Oklahoma 74155

Manuscript preparation and personalization of scriptures by
Betsy Williams, Tulsa, Oklahoma.

MAKING GOD'S WORD PERSONAL

I had what some might call a "crisis of faith," although that sounds a bit grand for a thirteen-year-old's first doubts.

Still, age has nothing to do with a crisis, and the subject was my faith. Perhaps it resulted from unanswered prayer. I had begged God (and my parents) to let me go home. Without success. Or it may have been spiritual growing pains. Like the young man who went to a delightfully sane bishop to confess he had lost his faith. "Nonsense," replied the bishop. "You've lost your parents' faith. Now go out and get one of your own." I knew God had sent His Son, Jesus, to die for the sins of mankind, but somehow I did not feel included. There were so many and I was only one and, let's face it, not a very significant one at that. I prayed for forgiveness and felt nothing. I wasn't even sure He was listening.

Finally, in desperation, I went to my ever-practical sister, Rosa, and asked her advice. "I don't know what to tell you to do," she replied matter-of-factly, "unless you take some verse and put your own name in. See if that helps." So I picked up my Bible and turned to Isaiah 53, one of my favorite chapters. I did just what she suggested—I read, "He was wounded for [Ruth's] transgressions, He was bruised for [Ruth's] iniquities: the chastisement of [Ruth's] peace was upon Him; and with His stripes [Ruth] is healed" (see Isaiah 53:5).

I knew then that I was included.[1]

—**Ruth Bell Graham**

---

[1] Ruth Bell Graham, *It's My Turn*, published by Fleming H. Revell, a division of Baker Book House Company, copyright 1982.

INTRODUCTION

What if all the great and glorious promises of God had your name written right on them? Well, they do! God meant every God-breathed word to be His personal message to *you*.

Here are some practical tools for your spiritual journey—precious promises that graduates need most, arranged under convenient topics. Each verse comes from the King James Bible, and whenever possible, we have carefully personalized the language either by using "I," "my," and "me" or by putting it into God's voice speaking to you. For example, *God has not given us a spirit of fear* has become *God, You have not given me the spirit of fear* or *"I have not given you the spirit of fear."* Experience the impact of God's love for you, the same way Ruth Bell Graham did as a young girl.

The additional affirmations, meditations, and Bible reading, as well as stories of great people in the Bible and their prayers will also uplift you as a graduate.

We pray that as you bring the Scripture into your daily life, God will empower you to become the man or woman you desire to be with a renewed sense of God's loving, *personal* commitment to you, His child. God bless you as you discover the protection and the power of God's promises to *you!*

TABLE OF CONTENTS

MY PERSONAL PROMISE BIBLE
FOR GRADUATES

HOW TO USE MY PERSONAL PROMISE BIBLE

Jesus said, "The words that I speak to you are spirit, and they are life" (John 6:63 NKJV). One of the most effective ways to experience a miraculous change in your life—the kind of change that will make you an even better person than you are now—is to allow God's words to sink deep into your heart through meditation, personalization of Scripture, and prayer. How?

Take a verse and memorize it. God's truth in you can then open your eyes to His great love for you. To get that truth to an even deeper, life-changing level, take that verse and think on it all day. Ask yourself, "How does this truth affect my life today?"

Next, make these promises personal. Any passage of Scripture can be personalized by inserting the personal pronouns *I, me,* and *my* into it, just as Ruth Bell Graham did. When you do this, God's truth becomes His truth *to you,* and you begin to experience lasting change in your life.

The final step is to pray these promises back to God. God's promises are His personal assurances to you. Not only will you be transformed by Him, you will become a spiritual encouragement in the lives of many others.

A CHRIST-LIKE HEART REFLECTS GOD'S . . .

*C*haracter in a saint means the
disposition of Jesus Christ
persistently manifested.

Oswald Chambers

We Christians have no veil over our faces;
we can be mirrors that brightly reflect
the glory of the Lord.
And as the Spirit of the Lord works within us,
we become more and more like him.

2 Corinthians 3:18 TLB

ACHIEVEMENT

*W*ithout counsel [my] purposes are disappointed, but in the multitude of counselors they are established.

Proverbs 15:22

Every purpose[even mine] is established by counsel.

Proverbs 20:18

His lord said to him, "Well done, you good and faithful servant. You have been faithful over a few things, I will make you ruler over many things. Enter into the joy of your lord."

Matthew 25:21

"Whatever your hand finds to do, do it with your might, for there is no work, nor device, nor knowledge, nor wisdom, in the grave, where you go."

Ecclesiastes 9:10

I do not count myself to have apprehended it, but this one thing I do, forgetting those things which are behind, and reaching forth to those things which are before, I press toward the mark for the prize of Your high calling, God, in Christ Jesus.

Philippians 3:13-14

ACHIEVEMENT

"As the rain comes down and the snow from heaven and does not return there but waters the earth, and makes it bring forth and bud, that it may give seed to the sower and bread to the eater; so shall My word be that goes forth out of My mouth. It shall not return to Me void, but it shall accomplish that which I please, and it shall prosper in the thing to where I send it."

Isaiah 55:10-11

Through wisdom is my house built, and by understanding it is established, and by knowledge shall the chambers be filled with all precious and pleasant riches.

Proverbs 24:3-4

There are many devices in a person's heart; nevertheless Your counsel, Lord, shall stand.

Proverbs 19:21

See a person diligent in their business? They shall stand before kings; they shall not stand before insignificant people.

Proverbs 22:29

ACHIEVEMENT

LORD, by wisdom You have founded the earth. By
understanding You have established the heavens.

Proverbs 3:19

"You have not chosen Me, but I have chosen you,
and ordained you, that you should go and bring forth
fruit, and that your fruit should remain, that whatever
you shall ask of the Father in My name, He may give it
to you."

John 15:16

"I am the vine, you are the branches. The one who
abides in Me, and I in him, the same brings forth
much fruit, for without Me you can do nothing."

John 15:5

Except You, LORD, build the house, they labor in vain
who build it. Except You, LORD, keep the city, the
watchman wake but in vain.

Psalm 127:1

*Four steps to achievement: Plan purposefully, prepare
prayerfully, proceed positively, pursue persistently.*

William Arthur Ward

A Christ-like Heart Reflects God's ...
COMMITMENT

Your mercy, LORD, is from everlasting to everlasting
upon me who fears You, and Your righteousness is unto
my children's children, to those who keep Your covenant
and remember Your commandments to do them.

Psalm 103:17-18

I am blessed because I keep Your testimonies and seek
You with my whole heart.

Psalm 119:2

Your eyes are upon the faithful of the land, that I
may dwell with You; if I walk in a perfect way, I shall
serve You.

Psalm 101:6

Your statutes, LORD, are right, rejoicing my heart.
Your commandment is pure, enlightening my eyes. . . .
Moreover by them I, Your servant, am warned, and
in keeping them there is great reward.

Psalm 19:8,11

"Commit your way unto Me, your LORD; trust also in
Me, and I shall bring it to pass."

Psalm 37:5

COMMITMENT

You honor me who fear You. I swear to my own hurt
and change not. . . . If I do these things I shall never
be moved.

Psalm 15:4-5

I love You, LORD, for You preserve me, the faithful, and
plentifully reward me, the proud doer.

Psalm 31:23

"Wait on Me, your LORD, and keep My way, and I
shall exalt you to inherit the land."

Psalm 37:34

All Your paths, LORD, are mercy and truth to me as I
keep Your covenant and Your testimonies.

Psalm 25:10

You shall keep me, O LORD; You shall preserve me
from this generation forever.

Psalm 12:7

Jesus is with me always, even unto the end of the world.

Matthew 28:20

*Keep me still established both in a constant assurance,
that you will speak to me at the beginning of every
such [soul] sickness, at the approach of every such sin;
and that, if I take knowledge of that voice then, and
fly to You, You will preserve me from falling, or raise
me again, when by natural infirmities I'm fallen.*

John Donne

COMPASSION

You will turn again, You will have compassion on me;
You will subdue my offenses, and You will cast all
my sins into the depths of the sea.

Micah 7:19

You have made Your wonderful works to be remem-
bered. You, LORD, are gracious and full of compassion.

Psalm 111:4

Because my heart is tender and I have humbled myself
before You, LORD, . . . You have heard me.

2 Kings 22:19

For me, the upright, there arises light in the darkness.
You are gracious, and full of compassion, and righteous.

Psalm 112:4

This I recall to my mind, therefore I have hope. It is of
Your mercies, LORD, that I am not consumed, because
Your compassions fail not. They are new every morning:
great is Your faithfulness.

Lamentations 3:21-22

COMPASSION

"Can a woman forget her sucking child, that she should not have compassion on the son of her womb? Behold I have engraved you on the palms of My hands; your walls are continually before Me."

Isaiah 49:15-16

It shall come to pass, after You have plucked us out, You will return and have compassion on me and will bring me again with every person to my heritage and with every person to my land.

Jeremiah 12:15

You, Lord, are very compassionate and of tender mercy.

James 5:11

You, O Lord, are a God full of compassion, and gracious, longsuffering, and plenteous in mercy and truth.

Psalm 86:15

I who have pity on the poor, lend to You, Lord; and that which I have given You will pay me again.

Proverbs 19:17

COMPASSION

If I shall return to You, the LORD my God, and shall
obey Your voice according to all that You command me
this day, me and my children, with all my heart and
with all my soul, then You, the Lord my God, will turn
my captivity and have compassion upon me. And You
will return and gather us from all the nations, wherever
You, the LORD our God, have scattered us.

Deuteronomy 30:2-3

"When you make a dinner or supper, call not your
friends, nor your brothers, neither your relatives nor
your rich neighbors; lest they also invite you again, and
a recompense be made to you. But when you make a
feast, call the poor, the maimed, the lame, the blind.
And you shall be blessed, for they cannot repay you. For
you shall be repaid at the resurrection of the just."

Luke 14:12-14

COMPASSION

If I turn again to You, LORD, my brothers and my
children shall find compassion . . . for You, the LORD
my God, are gracious and merciful, and will not turn
away Your face from me, if I return unto You.

2 Chronicles 30:9

God, You are not unrighteous to forget my work and
labor of love, which I have shown toward Your name,
in that I have ministered and continue to minister.

Hebrews 6:10

The mercies of God work compassion to others.
A Christian is a temporal savior. They feed the hungry,
clothe the naked, and visit the widow and orphan in their
distress; among them they sow the golden seeds of charity.

Thomas Watson

CONFIDENCE

I am not ashamed, for I know You, Jesus, whom I
have believed and am persuaded that You are able to
keep that which I have committed to You until that day.
                                          2 Timothy 1:12

"Cast not away, therefore, your confidence which has
great compensation of reward."
                                          Hebrews 10:35

Among the gods there is none like You, O Lord,
neither are there any works like Your works. . . . For
You are great and do wondrous things: You are God
alone. . . . For great is Your mercy toward me; and You
have delivered my soul from the lowest hell.
                                          Psalm 86:8,10,13

Who is God, except You, LORD? And who is a rock,
except You, my God? You are my strength and power,
and You make my way perfect.
                                          2 Samuel 22:32-33

CONFIDENCE

LORD, You shall be my confidence, and You shall keep my foot from being taken.

Proverbs 3:26

All things, whatever I shall ask in prayer, believing, I shall receive.

Matthew 21:22

Christ is a son over His own house, whose house I am, if I hold fast the confidence and the pride in the hope firm till the end.

Hebrews 3:6

In the fear of You, LORD, is strong confidence and Your children shall have a place of refuge.

Proverbs 14:26

The work of righteousness shall be peace; and the effect of righteousness [in my life] is quietness and assurance forever.

Isaiah 32:17

You have appointed a day in which You will judge the world in righteousness by that man [Christ] whom You have ordained. By this You have given assurance to all men and to me by raising Him from the dead.

Acts 17:31

CONFIDENCE

Our gospel came to you not in word only, but also in power and the Holy Spirit, and in much assurance.

1 Thessalonians 1:5

Having a high priest over the house of God, let me draw near with a true heart in full assurance of faith, having my heart sprinkled from an evil conscience and my body washed with pure water.

Hebrews 10:21-22

Let me therefore come boldly to the throne of grace that I may obtain mercy and find grace to help in time of need.

Hebrews 4:16

"If you abide in Me, and My words abide in you, you shall ask what you will, and it shall be done to you."

John 15:7

Now thanks be to You, God, who always causes me to triumph in Christ and makes manifest the savor of Your knowledge through me in every place.

2 Corinthians 2:14

CONFIDENCE

Being confident of this very thing, that You who have begun a good work in me will perform it until the day of Jesus Christ.

Philippians 1:6

Such trust I have through Christ of You, not that I am sufficient in myself to think anything as of myself, but my sufficiency is of You, God. You have made me an able minister of the new covenant.

2 Corinthians 3:4-6

Jesus Christ is the same yesterday, and today, and forever.

Hebrews 13:8

[Like Abraham,] I am fully persuaded that what You promised, You are able also to perform.

Romans 4:21

God wants us to be victors, not victims; to grow, not grovel; to soar, not sink; to overcome, not to be overwhelmed.

William Arthur Ward

COURAGE

*T*he exceeding greatness of Your power is to me who believes, according to the working of Your mighty power, which You wrought in Christ when You raised Him from the dead.

Ephesians 1:19-20

Praise You, LORD. I am blessed because I fear You, because I delight greatly in Your commandments. My seed shall be mighty upon the earth: my generation, the generation of the upright, shall be blessed.

Psalm 112:1-2

I deal courageously, and You, LORD, shall be with the good.

2 Chronicles 19:11

The weapons of my warfare are not carnal, but mighty through You, God, to the pulling down of strongholds; I cast down imaginations and every high thing that exalts itself against the knowledge of You, God, and bring every thought into captivity to the obedience of Christ.

2 Corinthians 10:4-5

COURAGE

Light arises to me, the upright, in the darkness. . . . I am not afraid of evil tidings: my heart is fixed, trusting in You, LORD.

Psalm 112:4,7

"These things I have spoken to you, that in Me you might have peace. In the world you shall have tribulation, but be of good cheer: I have overcome the world."

John 16:33

God, You have not given me the spirit of fear, but of power, and of love, and of a sound mind.

2 Timothy 1:7

I wait on You, LORD: I am of good courage, and You shall strengthen my heart. I wait, I say, on You.

Psalm 27:14

I am strong and very courageous, that I may observe to do according to all Your law. . . . I do not turn to the right hand or to the left, that I may prosper wherever I go.

Joshua 1:7

Through You, God, I shall do valiantly: for You shall tread down my enemies.

Psalm 60:12

His truth shall be my shield and buckler. I will not be afraid of the terror at night, nor for the arrow that flies by day, nor for the plague that walks in darkness, nor for the destruction that wastes at noon.

Psalm 91:4-6

31

COURAGE

LORD, You are on my side; I will not fear. What can man do to me? You are for me along with them that help me, therefore I shall see my desire upon those that hate me. It is better to trust in You than to put confidence in man.

Psalm 118:6-9

LORD, You shall help me and deliver me. You shall deliver me from the wicked and save me because I trust in You.

Psalm 37:40

I am strong and of good courage; I do not fear, nor am I afraid of them: for You, LORD my God, go with me; You will not fail me, nor forsake me.

Deuteronomy 31:6

My defense is from You, God, who save the upright in heart.

Psalm 7:10

Far better it is to dare mighty things, to win glorious triumphs, even though checkered by failure, than to take rank with those poor spirits who neither enjoy much nor suffer much because they live in the gray twilight that knows not victory nor defeat.

Theodore Roosevelt

EMPOWERMENT

God, You have spoken once, and twice I have heard that power belongs to You.

Psalm 62:11

I will sing of Your power. Yes, I will sing aloud of Your mercy in the morning, for You have been my defense and refuge in the day of my trouble.

Psalm 59:16

God, You have chosen the weak things of this world to shame the things that are mighty.

1 Corinthians 1:27

O God, You are awesome out of Your holy places. The God of Israel are You who give strength and power to Your people. Blessed be You, God.

Psalm 68:35

You rule by Your power forever. Your eyes behold the nations. Let not the rebellious exalt themselves.

Psalm 66:7

Touching the Almighty, we cannot find You out. You are excellent in power, and in judgment, and in plenty of justice. You will not afflict.

Job 37:23

EMPOWERMENT

"For My kingdom is not in words, but in power."

1 Corinthians 4:20

Great is my Lord, and of great power. His understanding is infinite.

Psalm 147:5

You give power to the faint; and to me who has no might, You increase strength.

Isaiah 40:29

[Paul wrote:] "We preach Christ crucified . . . to them who are called, both Jews and Greeks, Christ the power of God and the wisdom of God."

1 Corinthians 1:23-24

The preaching of the cross is foolishness to those who perish; but to me who is saved, it is Your power, God.

1 Corinthians 1:18

I have this treasure in an earthen vessel, that the excellency of the power may be of You, God, and not of myself.

2 Corinthians 4:7

Our Almighty Parent delights to conduct the tender nestlings of His care to the very edge of the precipice, and even to thrust them off into the steeps of air that they may learn their possession of unrealized power of flight, to be forever a luxury. And if, in the attempt, they be exposed to unwonted peril, He is prepared to swoop beneath them, and to bear them upward on His mighty pinions.

Lettie B. Cowman

ENCOURAGEMENT

*M*y liberal soul shall be made prosperous: and since I water, I shall be watered also myself.

Proverbs 11:25

Pleasant words [even mine] are as a honeycomb, sweet to the soul, and health to the bones.

Proverbs 16:24

I will speak of excellent things and the opening of my lips shall reveal right things, for my mouth shall speak truth.

Proverbs 8:6-7

I am poor and needy; make haste unto me, O God. You are my help and my deliverer; O LORD, do not tarry.

Psalm 70:5

I will remember Your works, LORD. Surely I will remember Your wonders of old. I will meditate also on all Your work and talk of Your doings. . . . You are the God who does wonders. You have declared Your strength among the people.

Psalm 77:11-12,14

Encouragement

Lord GOD, You have given me the tongue of the learned, that I should know how to speak a word in season to one who is weary.

Isaiah 50:4

LORD, You are near to me because I call upon You; I call upon You in truth. You will fulfill my desire because I fear You. You also will hear my cry and will save me.

Psalm 145:18-19

My enemy should not rejoice against me, because when I fall, I shall arise; when I sit in darkness, the LORD shall be a Light unto me.

Micah 7:8

A word fitly spoken [by me] is like apples of gold in pictures of silver.

Proverbs 25:11

You, LORD, will regard my prayer when I am destitute and not despise my prayer.

Psalm 102:17

Once I heard a beautiful prayer, which I can never forget. It was this: "Lord, take my lips and speak through them; take my mind and think through it; take my heart and set it on fire." And this is the way the Master keeps the lips of His servants—by so filling their hearts with His love that the outflow cannot be unloving.

Frances Ridley Havergal

FAITH

*G*od, You have dealt to me, and every person, the
measure of faith.

Romans 12:3

"Trust in Me, Your LORD, with all your heart; and lean
not on your own understanding. In all your ways,
acknowledge Me, and I will direct your paths."

Proverbs 3:5-6

[Paul's] speech and his preaching were not with enticing
words of man's wisdom but in demonstration of Your
Spirit and of power, that my faith should not stand in
the wisdom of men but in Your power, God.

1 Corinthians 2:4-5

"Have faith in Me. . . . Whatever things you desire,
when you pray, believe that you receive them, and you
shall have them."

Mark 11:22,24

The effectual fervent prayers of the righteous avail much.

James 5:16

My faith comes by hearing, and hearing by Your
word, God.

Romans 10:17

FAITH

I am crucified with Christ, nevertheless I live; yet not I but Christ lives in me. And the life which I now live in the flesh, I live by the faith of the Son of God, who loved me and gave Himself for me.

Galatians 2:20

Above all, I'm taking the shield of faith, with which I shall be able to quench all the fiery darts of the wicked.

Ephesians 6:16

By grace I am saved through faith, and that not of myself; it is Your gift, God.

Ephesians 2:8

Jesus Christ, whom having not seen, I love; in whom, though now I do not see Him, yet believing, I rejoice with joy unspeakable and full of glory, receiving the end of my faith, even the salvation of my soul.

1 Peter 1:7-9

FAITH

If I have faith as a grain of mustard seed, I shall say to this mountain, Remove from here to yonder place, and it shall move; and nothing shall be impossible to me.

Matthew 17:20

Whatever I shall ask of You, Father, in Jesus' name, You will give it to me. . . . I ask and I shall receive, that my joy may be full.

John 16:23-24

Without faith it is impossible to please You, for he who comes to You must believe that You are and that You are a rewarder of those who diligently seek You.

Hebrews 11:6

[Jesus said,] "The one who believes on Me, the works that I do shall he do also, and greater works than these shall he do, because I go to My Father."

John 14:12

The just shall live by my faith.

Habakkuk 2:4

FAITH

"If you can believe, all things are possible to you who believe. . . ." Lord, I believe; help my unbelief.

Mark 9:23-24

Whatever is born of You, God, overcomes the world; and this is the victory that overcomes the world, even my faith.

1 John 5:4

Now the righteousness of God without the law is manifested, being witnessed by the law and the prophets; even the righteousness of God which is by faith in Jesus Christ to all and upon all those who believe: for there is no difference.

Romans 3:21-22

The Word is the instrumental cause of our conversion, the Spirit is the efficient . . . it is the Spirit blowing in them, that effectually changes the heart. . . . Therefore the aid of God's Spirit is to be implored, that He would put forth His powerful voice, and awaken us out of the grave of unbelief.

Thomas Watson

FORGIVENESS

*"J*udge not, and you shall not be judged. Condemn not, and you shall not be condemned. Forgive, and you shall be forgiven."

Luke 6:37

Great peace I have who love Your law, and nothing shall offend me.

Psalm 119:165

I confess my faults to others and pray for others, that I may be healed.

James 5:16

Giving thanks to You, Father, who has . . . translated us into the kingdom of Your dear Son, in whom I have redemption through His blood, even the forgiveness of sins.

Colossians 1:12-14

I, being dead in my sins . . . You have quickened together with Jesus, having forgiven me all offenses, blotting out the note of debt that was against me, which was antagonistic to me. You took it out of the way, nailing it to Jesus' cross.

Colossians 2:13-14

FORGIVENESS

"When you stand praying, forgive if you have anything
against anyone, that your Father also who is in heaven,
may forgive you your offenses."

Mark 11:25

The Son of man has power on earth to forgive my sins.

Luke 5:24

"Be it known to you therefore, . . . that through this
man is preached to you the forgiveness of sins: And by
Him all that believe are justified from all things, from
which you could not be justified by the law of Moses."

Acts 13:38-39

I have redemption through His blood, the forgiveness
of sins, according to the riches of His grace.

Ephesians 1:7

If I forgive others their offense, You, my heavenly
Father, will also forgive me.

Matthew 6:14

Blessed is the one whose offenses are forgiven and
whose sins are covered. Blessed is the one to whom the
Lord will not impute sin.

Romans 4:7

Forgiveness

Put on . . . longsuffering, bearing with others and
forgiving them if you have a quarrel against anyone;
even as Christ forgave you, so you also forgive.

Colossians 3:13

As far as the east is from the west, so far You have
removed my transgressions from me.

Psalm 103:12

"'Come now, and let us reason together,' says the LORD.
'Though your sins are as scarlet, they shall be as white
as snow. Though they are red like crimson, they shall
be as wool.'"

Isaiah 1:18

"I am He who blots out your transgressions for my
own sake and will not remember your sins. Put me in
remembrance; let us plead together. Speak, that you
may be justified."

Isaiah 43:25-26

It is cheaper to pardon than to resent.
Forgiveness saves the expense of anger,
the cost of hatred.

Hannah More

FREEDOM

*C*reation itself also shall be delivered from the bondage of corruption into the glorious liberty of the children of God.

Romans 8:21

[Jesus said,] "The Spirit of the Lord is upon Me, because He has anointed Me . . . to set at liberty those who are bruised."

Luke 4:18

[If I] look into the perfect law of liberty and continue in it, I, being not a forgetful hearer but a doer of the work, I shall be blessed in my deed.

James 1:25

I have been called to liberty, only I am not to use liberty for an occasion to indulge the flesh, but by love I am to serve others.

Galatians 5:13

"Stand fast in the liberty with which Christ has made you free, and do not be entangled again with the yoke of bondage."

Galatians 5:1

FREEDOM

If the Son shall make me free, I shall be free indeed.

John 8:36

I shall know the truth, and the truth will make me free.

John 8:32

I will walk at liberty, for I seek Your precepts.

Psalm 119:45

Restore to me the joy of Your salvation, and uphold me with Your free Spirit.

Psalm 51:12

I, who was baptized into Jesus Christ, was baptized into His death; therefore, I am buried with Him by baptism into death. Likewise, as Christ was raised up from the dead by the glory of the Father, even so I also should walk in newness of life . . . knowing this, that my old man is crucified with Him, that the body of sin might be destroyed, that from now on I should no longer serve sin. For the one who is dead is freed from sin.

Romans 6:3-4,6-7

FREEDOM

Though I am free from all men, yet I have made myself
servant to all, that I might gain more.

1 Corinthians 9:19

Being made free from sin, I became the servant
of righteousness.

Romans 6:18

"Take heed lest by any means this liberty of yours
becomes a stumbling block to those who are weak."

1 Corinthians 8:9

Where the Spirit of the Lord is, there is liberty
[for me].

2 Corinthians 3:17

I called upon You, LORD, in distress; You, LORD,
answered me and set me in a large place.

Psalm 118:5

The law of the Spirit of life in Christ Jesus has made
me free from the law of sin and death.

Romans 8:2

*Christ has once again made you free from the power
of sin, as well as from its guilt and punishment. So do
not become entangled again in the yoke of bondage. . . .
If you have stumbled, O seeker of God, do not
just lie there fretting and bemoaning your weakness!
Patiently pray: "Lord, I acknowledge that every moment
I would be stumbling if You were not upholding me."
And then get up! Leap! Walk! Go on your way!*

John Wesley

Friendship

"*M*ake no friendship with an angry person, and with a furious person you shall not go, lest you learn their ways and get a snare to your soul."

Proverbs 22:24

A person who has friends must show themselves friendly, and there is a friend who sticks closer than a brother.

Proverbs 18:24

The person who loves pureness of heart, for the grace of their lips the king shall be their friend.

Proverbs 22:11

A friend loves at all times, and a brother is born for adversity.

Proverbs 17:17

Friendship of the world is enmity with You, God. Whoever therefore would be a friend of the world is Your enemy.

James 4:4

Abraham believed You, and it was counted for him as righteousness, and he was called Your friend, God.

James 2:23

FRIENDSHIP

Iron sharpens iron, so a person sharpens the countenance of his friend.

Proverbs 27:17

Your own friend and your father's friend, do not forsake; neither go into your brother's house in the day of your calamity. Better is a neighbor who is near than a brother far off.

Proverbs 27:10

Faithful are the wounds of a friend, but the kisses of an enemy are deceitful.

Proverbs 27:6

[Jesus said,] "From now on I do not call you servants, for the servant does not know what his lord does, but I have called you friends, for all things that I have heard of My Father I have made known to you."

John 15:15

A friend is one who knows you as you are,
understands where you've been,
accepts who you've become,
and still, gently, invites you to grow.

Unknown

GUIDANCE

"*Y*our ears will hear a word behind you, saying, 'This is the way, walk in it, when you turn to the right hand, and when you turn to the left.'"

Isaiah 30:21

"You will not go out with haste, nor go by flight; for the LORD will go before you; and I, the God of Israel, will be your rear guard."

Isaiah 52:12

You will show me the path of life; in Your presence is fullness of joy; at Your right hand there are pleasures forevermore.

Psalm 16:11

I will instruct you and teach you in the way which you shall go. I will guide you with my eye.

Psalm 32:8

A person's heart devises their way, but You, LORD, direct their steps [even mine].

Proverbs 16:9

"In all your ways acknowledge Him, and He will direct your paths."

Proverbs 3:6

GUIDANCE

Your word is a lamp to my feet and a light to my path.
Psalm 119:105

I have an anointing from the Holy One, and I know
all things.
1 John 2:20

The righteousness of the blameless will direct their way;
but the wicked will fall by their own wickedness.
Proverbs 11:57

There are many devices in a person's heart; nevertheless
Your counsel, LORD, will stand.
Proverbs 19:21

[Paul wrote:] "We . . . do not cease to pray for you, and
to desire that you might be filled with the knowledge of
His will in all wisdom and spiritual understanding, that
you might walk worthy of the Lord to all pleasing,
being fruitful in every good work, and increasing in the
knowledge of God . . . giving thanks to the Father, who
has made us meet to be partakers of the inheritance of
the saints in light."
Colossians 1:9–10,12

Guidance

You, God, are my God forever and ever. You will be my
guide even to death.

Psalm 48:14

The meek You will guide in judgment; and the meek
You will teach Your way.

Psalm 25:9

The path of the just is as the shining light, that shines
more and more until the perfect day.

Proverbs 4:18

"The sheep hear [the shepherd's] voice, and he calls his
own sheep by name, and leads them out. And when he
puts forth his own sheep, he goes before them, and the
sheep follow him, for they know his voice. And a
stranger they will not follow, but will flee from him, for
they do not know the voice of strangers. . . . My sheep
hear My voice, and I know them, and they follow Me."

John 10:3-5,27

LORD, You lead me in the paths of righteousness for
Your name's sake.

Psalm 23:3

GUIDANCE

"When He, the Spirit of truth, is come, He will guide you into all truth, for He shall not speak of Himself, but whatever He shall hear, that shall He speak, and He will show you things to come."

John 16:13

"I will bring the blind by a way that they did not know; I will lead you in paths that you have not known; I will make darkness light before you and crooked things straight. These things I will do for you and not forsake you."

Isaiah 42:16

You are my rock and my fortress; therefore for Your name's sake lead me, and guide me.

Psalm 31:3

"Thus says the LORD, your Redeemer, the Holy One of Israel: 'I am the LORD Your God who teaches you to profit, who leads you by the way that you should go.'"

Isaiah 48:17

God gives us his light in an instant, allowing us to know all that we need to know. No more is given to us than is necessary in his plan to lead us to perfection. We cannot seek this light; it is given to us from God only as he chooses. Neither do we know how it comes, or how we even know that it is! If we try to know more than we have been made to know, we will accomplish nothing.

Catherine of Genoa

HOPE

*N*ow the God of hope fill me with all joy and peace in believing, that I may abound in hope, through the power of the Holy Spirit.

Romans 15:13

Whatever things were written before were written for my learning, that I through patience and comfort of the scriptures might have hope.

Romans 15:4

The mystery, which has been hidden from ages and from generations but now is made manifest to Your saints, . . . is Christ in us, the hope of glory.

Colossians 1:26-27

If in this life only, we have hope in Christ, we are of all men most miserable. But now Christ is risen from the dead.

1 Corinthians 15:19-20

Remember the word to Your servant upon which You have caused me to hope. This is my comfort in my affliction, for Your word has revived me.

Psalm 119:49-50

HOPE

Your eye, LORD, is upon me who fears You, upon me
who hopes in Your mercy, to deliver my soul from death
and to keep me alive in famine.

Psalm 33:18-19

"The LORD is my portion," says my soul, "therefore I
will hope in Him." You, LORD, are good to me who
waits for You, to the soul who seeks You. It is good
that I should both hope and quietly wait for Your
salvation, LORD.

Lamentations 3:24-26

In You, LORD, do I hope; You will hear, O Lord
my God.

Psalm 38:15

Being justified by Your grace, I should be made an heir
according to the hope of eternal life.

Titus 3:7

My soul waits for You, LORD. You are my help and my
shield. For my heart will rejoice in You, because I have
trusted in Your holy name. Let Your mercy, O LORD,
be upon me, according as I hope in You.

Psalm 33:20-22

Hope

By [my Lord Jesus Christ] I also have access by faith into this grace in which I stand, and I rejoice in hope of the glory of God.

Romans 5:2

You are my hope, O Lord GOD. You are my trust from my youth. . . . I will hope continually and will yet praise You more and more.

Psalm 71:5,14

I am saved by hope, but hope that is seen is not hope. For if one sees, why does he yet hope for it? But if I hope for that which I do not see, then I do patiently wait for it.

Romans 8:24-25

[Paul wrote:] "We heard of your faith in Christ Jesus, and of the love that you have for all the saints because of the hope which is laid up for you in heaven."

Colossians 1:4-5

HOPE

More abundantly willing to show to the heirs of
promise [and to me], the unchangeability of Your
counsel, You confirmed it by an oath, that by two
unchangeable things, in which it was impossible for You
to lie, I, who have fled for refuge, might have a strong
consolation to lay hold upon the hope set before me,
which hope I have as an anchor of my soul, both sure
and steadfast.

Hebrews 6:17-19

I have set You, LORD, always before me; because You
are at my right hand, I shall not be moved. Therefore
my heart is glad, and my glory rejoices; my flesh also
shall rest in hope.

Psalm 16:8-9

Why are you cast down, O my soul? And why are you
disquieted within me? Hope in God. I shall yet praise
Him who is the health of my countenance and my God.

Psalm 42:11

HOPE

Those who fear You will be glad when they see me,
because I have hoped in Your word.

Psalm 119:74

As the sufferings of Christ abound in me, so my
consolation also abounds by Christ.

2 Corinthians 1:5

I was without Christ, an alien from the commonwealth
of Israel and a stranger from the covenants of promise,
having no hope and without God, in the world. But
now in Christ Jesus, I, who sometimes was far off, am
made near by the blood of Christ.

Ephesians 2:12-13

O hope! Dazzling, radiant hope!
What a change thou bringest to the hopeless;
brightening the darkened paths,
and cheering the lonely way.

Aimee Semple McPherson

INTEGRITY

*T*he LORD shall judge the people; judge me, O LORD, according to my righteousness and according to my integrity that is in me. Oh let the wickedness of the wicked come to an end, but establish the just, for You, the righteous God, try the minds and hearts. My defense is of God, who saves the upright in heart.

Psalm 7:8-10

I who speak truth show forth righteousness. . . . Lying lips are an abomination to You, LORD, but I who deal truly am Your delight.

Proverbs 12:17,22

Your word, LORD, is right, and all Your works are done in truth. You love righteousness and judgment. The earth is full of Your goodness, LORD.

Psalm 33:4-5

My mouth, the mouth of the just, brings forth wisdom, but the perverse tongue shall be cut out.

Proverbs 10:31

The one who walks uprightly walks surely, but the one who perverts their ways shall be known.

Proverbs 10:9

INTEGRITY

The integrity of the upright will guide me, but the
perverseness of transgressors will destroy them.

Proverbs 11:3

You are the Rock, Your work is perfect, for all Your
ways are judgment, a God of truth and without sin, just
and right are You.

Deuteronomy 32:4

You shall cover me with Your feathers, and under
Your wings I shall trust. Your truth shall be my shield
and buckler.

Psalm 91:4

Behold, You desire truth in the inward parts, and in the
hidden part You shall make me to know wisdom.

Psalm 51:6

Righteousness keeps me who is upright in the way, but
wickedness overthrows the sinner.

Proverbs 13:6

*A person who lives right and is right has more power in his
silence than another has by words. Character is like bells,
which ring out sweet notes and which, when touched—
accidentally even—resound with sweet music.*

Phillips Brooks

JOY

*T*he meek also shall increase their joy in You, LORD, and the poor among men shall rejoice in the Holy One of Israel.

Isaiah 29:19

You have turned for me my mourning into dancing. You have put off my sackcloth, and girded me with gladness, to the end that my glory may sing praise to thee, and not be silent.

Psalm 30:11-12

You make the barren woman to keep house and to be a joyful mother of children.

Psalm 113:9

[Jesus said,] "If you keep My commandments, you shall abide in My love; even as I have kept My Father's commandments and abide in His love. These things I have spoken to you that My joy might remain in you and that your joy might be full."

John 15:10-11

JOY

A merry heart makes a cheerful countenance, but by
sorrow of the heart the spirit is broken.

Proverbs 15:13

All the days of the afflicted are evil, but a merry heart
[even mine] has a continual feast.

Proverbs 15:15

I shall go out with joy and be led forth with peace.
The mountains and the hills shall break forth before
me into singing, and all the trees of the field shall clap
their hands.

Isaiah 55:12

Your kingdom, God, is not meat and drink, but righteousness, and peace, and joy in the Holy Spirit.

Romans 14:17

You will show me the path of life. In Your presence
is fullness of joy. At Your right hand there are
pleasures forever.

Psalm 16:11

I also joy in You, God, through my Lord Jesus Christ,
by whom I have now received the atonement.

Romans 5:11

Joy

My merry heart does good like a medicine, but a broken spirit dries the bones.

Proverbs 17:22

You, LORD, have made me glad through Your work; I will triumph in the works of Your hands. O LORD, how great are Your works! And Your thoughts are very deep.

Psalm 92:4-5

My soul shall make her boast in You, LORD; the humble shall hear of it and be glad.

Psalm 34:2

The joy of the LORD is my strength.

Nehemiah 8:10

Eternal bliss is rooted in God alone and nothing else. And if people are to be saved, this one and only God must be in their soul. . . . For bliss or blessedness does not come from the wealth of things, but from God. In other words, bliss or blessedness does not depend on any created thing or on a creature's work, but only on God and His works.

Theologia Germanica

LEADERSHIP

*M*y voice shall You hear in the morning, O LORD. In the morning will I direct my prayer to You, and will look up. . . . Lead me, O LORD, in Your righteousness because of my enemies. Make my way straight before my face.

Psalm 5:3,8

LORD, You are my shepherd. I shall not want. . . . You lead me beside the still waters. . . . You lead me in the paths of righteousness for Your name's sake.

Psalm 23:1-3

From the end of the earth will I cry to You, when my heart is overwhelmed. Lead me to the rock that is higher than I. For You have been a shelter for me, and a strong tower from the enemy.

Psalm 61:2-3

You are my rock and my fortress; therefore, for Your name's sake lead me, and guide me.

Psalm 31:3

LEADERSHIP

O LORD, You have searched me and known me. You
know my sitting down and my uprising. You understand
my thoughts from far away. . . . Where shall I go from
Your Spirit? Or where shall I flee from Your presence?
If I ascend up into heaven, You are there. If I make my
bed in hell, behold, You are there. If I take the wings of
the morning, and dwell in the uttermost parts of the
sea, even there shall Your hand lead me, and Your right
hand shall hold me.

Psalm 139:1-2,7-10

Cause me to hear Your lovingkindness in the morning,
for in You do I trust. Cause me to know the way in
which I should walk, for I lift up my soul to You. . . .
Teach me to do Your will, for You are my God. Your
Spirit is good. Lead me into the land of uprightness.

Psalm 143:8,10

LEADERSHIP

Lord GOD, You will come with strong hand, and Your
arm shall rule for You. Behold, Your reward is with You,
and Your work before You. You shall feed Your flock
like a shepherd. You shall gather the lambs with Your
arm, and carry them in Your bosom, and shall gently
lead those who are with young.

Isaiah 40:10-11

"I, [the LORD], will bring the blind by a way that they
did not know. I will lead them in paths that they have
not known. I will make darkness light before them and
crooked things straight."

Isaiah 42:16

"Thus says the LORD, your Redeemer, the Holy One of
Israel: 'I am the LORD your God who teaches you to
profit, who leads you by the way that you should go.'"

Isaiah 48:17

Do not lead us into temptation, but deliver us from
evil, for Yours is the kingdom, and the power, and the
glory, forever.

Matthew 6:13

LEADERSHIP

Lead me in Your truth, and teach me, for You are the God of my salvation. On You do I wait all the day.

Psalm 25:5

"Behold, I, God, have given Him for a witness to the people, a leader and commander to the people."

Isaiah 55:4

"My child, keep your father's commandment, and do not forsake the law of your mother. Bind them continually on your heart and tie them about your neck. When you go, it shall lead you. When you sleep, it shall keep you, and when you awake, it shall talk with you. For the commandment is a lamp, and the law is light."

Proverbs 6:20-23

"I, [Wisdom] lead in the way of righteousness, in the midst of the paths of judgment, that I may cause those who love me to inherit substance, and I will fill their treasures."

Proverbs 8:20-21

Do you wish to rise? Begin by descending.
You plan a tower that shall pierce the clouds?
Lay first the foundation of humility!

Augustine of Hippo

LOVE

*H*atred stirs up strifes, but love covers all sins.

Proverbs 10:12

I know that I have passed from death to life, because I love the brethren.

1 John 3:14

Love is long-suffering and kind; it does not envy . . . it is not puffed up, it does not behave itself unbecomingly, it does not seek its own way, is not easily provoked, thinks no evil; it does not rejoice in wrongdoing but rejoices in the truth; it bears all things, believes all things, hopes all things, endures all things. Love never fails.

1 Corinthians 13:4-8

"Love your enemies and do good and lend, hoping for nothing in return; and your reward will be great; you shall be the children of the Highest; for I am kind to the unthankful and to the evil."

Luke 6:35

LOVE

He who does not love, does not know God; for You, God, are love.

1 John 4:8

[Jesus said,] "A new commandment I give to you, that you love one another. As I have loved you, you also love one another. By this shall all men know that you are My disciples, if you have love one to another."

John 13:34-35

I am persuaded that neither death, nor life, nor angels, nor principalities, nor powers, nor things present, nor things to come, nor height, nor depth, nor any other creature, will be able to separate me from the love of God, which is in Christ Jesus my Lord.

Romans 8:38-39

You, LORD, will command Your loving kindness in the daytime, and in the night Your song shall be with me, and my prayer to the God of my life.

Psalm 42:8

Love

O LORD God of Israel, there is no God like You in the heaven, nor in the earth, who keeps covenant and shows mercy to Your servants, who walk before You with all their hearts.

2 Chronicles 6:14

The one who spares the rod hates their child; but if I love my children I will promptly discipline them.

Proverbs 13:24

Above all these things put on love, which is the bond of perfection.

Colossians 3:14

God, You are rich in mercy. Because of Your great love with which You loved me, even when I was dead in sins, You have made us alive together with Christ, (by grace I am saved).

Ephesians 2:4-5

I perceive Your love, God, because You laid down Your life for me. And I ought to lay down my life for the brethren.

1 John 3:16

LOVE

Hope does not make ashamed, because the love of God is shed abroad in my heart by the Holy Spirit, who is given to me.

Romans 5:5

Behold what manner of love the Father has bestowed on me, that we should be called the children of God; therefore the world knows us not, because it knew Him not.

1 John 3:1

God loved me so much that He gave His only begotten Son, that whoever believes in Him [including me] shall not perish, but will have everlasting life.

John 3:16

I have known and believed the love that God has for me. God is love; and I who dwell in love, dwell in God, and God dwells in me.

1 John 4:16

I love Him, because He first loved me.

1 John 4:19

LOVE

"Thus says the LORD, 'Yes, I have loved you with an everlasting love, therefore with lovingkindness I have drawn you.'"

Jeremiah 31:3

Let us love one another, for love is of God, and everyone who loves is born of God and knows God.

1 John 4:7

May [I] be able to comprehend with all saints what is the breadth, and length, and depth, and height; and to know the love of Christ which passes knowledge, that I might be filled with all Your fullness, God.

Ephesians 3:18-20

One will scarcely die for a righteous man, yet perhaps for a good man some would even dare to die. But, God, You commend Your love toward me, in that while I was yet a sinner, Christ died for me.

Romans 5:7-8

Let your religion be less of a theory and more of a love affair.

G. K. Chesterton

71

LOYALTY

You honor those who fear You, LORD—one who swears to his own hurt and does not change.

Psalm 15:4

"I have said, 'I will never leave you, nor forsake you.'"

Hebrews 13:5

No one has greater love than this, that one lay down their life for their friends.

John 15:13

Is not this the fast that I have chosen? . . . that you not hide yourself from your own family? Then shall thy light break forth as the morning, and thine health shall spring forth speedily: and thy righteousness shall go before thee; the glory of the LORD shall be thy reward.

Isaiah 58:6-7

[Love] thinks no evil, does not rejoice in wrongdoing, but rejoices in the truth; bears all things, believes all things, hopes all things, endures all things. [Love] never fails.

1 Corinthians 13:5-8

I will speak ill of no man and speak
all the good I know of everybody.

Benjamin Franklin

A CHRIST-LIKE HEART REFLECTS GOD'S . . .
MERCY

*B*y mercy and truth sin is purged.

Proverbs 16:6

Not by works of righteousness which I have done, but
according to Your mercy You saved me, by the washing
of regeneration and renewing of the Holy Spirit.

Titus 3:5

Blessed be the God and Father of my Lord Jesus
Christ, who according to His abundant mercy has
begotten me again to a lively hope by the resurrection
of Jesus Christ from the dead.

1 Peter 1:3

I have a great high priest . . . Jesus the Son of God. . . .
I do not have a high priest who cannot be touched
with the feeling of my infirmities. . . . Let me, therefore,
come boldly to the throne of grace, that I may obtain
mercy and find grace to help in time of need.

Hebrews 4:14-16

MERCY

Mercy and truth preserve the king, and his throne is
upheld by mercy.

Proverbs 20:28

The one who despises their neighbor sins, but if I have
mercy on the poor I am happy.

Proverbs 14:21

I will not hunger nor thirst, nor will the heat nor the
sun smite me, for You who have mercy on me will lead
me, even by the springs of water will You guide me.

Isaiah 49:10

Sow to yourselves in righteousness, reap in mercy; break
up your fallow ground, for it is time to seek the LORD,
till He come and rain righteousness upon you.

Hosea 10:12

Through the tender mercy of my God, the dayspring
from on high has visited me, to give light to me who
sits in darkness and in the shadow of death, to guide
my feet into the way of peace.

Luke 1:78-79

Mercy

"Jacob had power over My angel, and prevailed: he
wept, and prayed to him . . . and there I spoke with you;
Even I, the LORD God of hosts; I, the LORD, am his
memorial [to you]. Therefore turn to Me: keep mercy
and judgment, and wait on Me, your God, continually."

Hosea 12:4-6

Blessed am I, the merciful, for I shall obtain mercy.

Matthew 5:7

Let me return to You, LORD, and You will have
mercy on me; and to You, God, for You will
abundantly pardon.

Isaiah 55:7

"Be merciful, as your Father also is merciful. Judge
not, and you shall not be judged. Condemn not, and
you shall not be condemned. Forgive, and you shall
be forgiven."

Luke 6:36-37

"Let not mercy and truth forsake you. Bind them about
your neck; write them upon the table of your heart, so
shall you find favor and good understanding in the sight
of God and man."

Proverbs 3:3-4

MERCY

I who follow after righteousness and mercy find life,
righteousness, and honor.

Proverbs 21:21

Your mercy is on those who fear You, from generation
to generation.

Luke 1:50

LORD, You are merciful and gracious, slow to anger
and plenteous in mercy.

Psalm 103:8

O LORD God of heaven, the great and terrible God,
who keeps covenant and mercy for me who loves You
and observes Your commandments, let Your ear now
be attentive and Your eyes open.

Nehemiah 1:5-6

You have shown me . . . what is good; and what do You,
LORD, require of me but to do justly and to love mercy
and to walk humbly with You, my God?

Micah 6:8

Remember, O LORD, Your tender mercies and Your
loving kindnesses, for they have been ever of old.

Psalm 25:6

Mercy comes down from heaven to earth
so that one, by practicing it, may resemble God.

Giambattista Giraldi

OPTIMISM

*G*od, You are light, and in You is no darkness at all.

1 John 1:5

We know that all things work together for good to those who love You, God, to those who are called according to Your purpose.

Romans 8:28

I will lift up my eyes to the hills, from where comes my help. My help comes from You, LORD, who made heaven and earth.

Psalm 121:1-2

I know both how to be abased, and I know how to abound. Everywhere and in all things I am instructed both to be full and to be hungry, both to abound and to suffer need. I can do all things through Christ who strengthens me.

Philippians 4:12

God, You are able to make all grace abound toward me, that I, always having all sufficiency in all things, may abound to every good work.

2 Corinthians 9:8

OPTIMISM

Rejoice in the Lord always, and again I say, "Rejoice."
. . . The Lord is at hand.

Philippians 4:4,6

Thanks be to You, God, who always causes me to
triumph in Christ, and makes manifest the savor of
Your knowledge by me in every place.

2 Corinthians 2:14

My voice shall You hear in the morning, O LORD. In
the morning will I direct my prayer to You, and will
look up.

Psalm 5:3

"Then shall they see the Son of man coming in a cloud
with power and great glory. And when these things
begin to come to pass, then look up, and lift up your
heads, for your redemption draws near."

Luke 21:27–28

You will light my candle. You, LORD my God, will
enlighten my darkness. For by You I have run through a
troop, and by You, my God, have I leaped over a wall.

Psalm 18:28-29

All things shall be well and all shall be well,
and all manner of things shall be well.

Julian of Norwich

PEACE

"*Peace* I leave with you, my peace I give to you, not as the world gives do I give to you. Do not let your heart be troubled, neither let it be afraid."

John 14:27

LORD, You are my shepherd. I shall not want. You make me to lie down in green pastures. You lead me beside the still waters.

Psalm 23:1-2

You have delivered my soul in peace from the battle that was against me, for there were many with me.

Psalm 55:18

All things are of God, who has reconciled me to Himself by Jesus Christ and has given to me the ministry of reconciliation. To wit, that God was in Christ, reconciling me to Himself, not counting my sins against me, and He has committed to me the word of reconciliation.

2 Corinthians 5:18-19

PEACE

"The work of righteousness shall be peace, and the effect of righteousness quietness and assurance forever. And My people shall dwell in a peaceable habitation and in sure dwellings, and in quiet resting places."

Isaiah 32:17-18

"Don't worry about anything, but in everything by prayer and supplication with thanksgiving, let your requests be made known to Me. And My peace, which passes all understanding, will keep your heart and mind through Christ Jesus."

Philippians 4:6-7

Great peace have I who love Your law, and nothing shall offend me.

Psalm 119:165

If when we were enemies, I was reconciled to God, by the death of His Son, much more, being reconciled, I shall be saved by His life.

Romans 5:10

"Be still and know that I am God. I will be exalted among the heathen; I will be exalted in the earth."

Psalm 46:10

PEACE

[The apostle Paul wrote:] "Do those things, which you have both learned, and received, and heard and seen in me, and the God of peace will be with you."

Philippians 4:9

Being justified by faith, we have peace with God through our Lord Jesus Christ.

Romans 5:1

To be carnally minded is death, but to be spiritually minded [for me] is life and peace.

Romans 8:6

"'The mountains will depart, and the hills be removed, but My kindness will not depart from you, neither will the covenant of My peace be removed,' says the LORD who has mercy on you."

Isaiah 54:10

The punishment for my peace was upon You, Jesus.

Isaiah 53:5

Mark the perfect person and behold the upright, for the end of that person shall be peace.

Psalm 37:37

Peace

"I am not the author of confusion but of peace as in all churches of the saints."

1 Corinthians 14:33

Blessed are the peacemakers, for they shall be called children of God.

Matthew 5:9

Deceit is in the heart of those who imagine evil, but to the counselors of peace is joy.

Proverbs 12:20

You will keep me in perfect peace, whose mind is stayed on You, because I trust in You.

Isaiah 26:3

"'I create the fruit of the lips; Peace, peace to him that is far off and to you who are near, and I will heal you,' says the LORD."

Isaiah 57:19

The fruit of righteousness is sown in peace by me who makes peace.

James 3:18

True peace is found by man in the depths of his own heart, the dwelling-place of God.

Johann Tauler

PERSEVERANCE

[*P*aul wrote:] "Stand fast and hold the traditions that you have been taught, whether by word or by the epistles. Now our Lord Jesus Christ Himself and God, even our Father, who has loved you and has given you everlasting consolation and good hope through grace comfort your heart and establish you in every good word and work."

2 Thessalonians 2:15-17

"Stand fast, therefore, in the liberty with which I, Christ, have made you free, and do not be entangled again with the yoke of bondage."

Galatians 5:1

[James said:] "We count them happy who endure [even you]. You have heard of the patience of Job, and have seen the end of the Lord; that the Lord is very pitiful, and of tender mercy."

James 5:11

"Wait on Me, your LORD. Be of good courage, and I will strengthen your heart. Wait, I say, on Me."

Psalm 27:14

PERSEVERANCE

"Be sober, be vigilant because your adversary the devil, as a roaring lion, walks about, seeking whom he may devour. Resist him, steadfast in the faith, knowing that the same afflictions are accomplished by your fellow believers who are in the world."

1 Peter 5:8-9

"You be steadfast, immovable, always abounding in My work, inasmuch as you know that your labor is not in vain in the Lord."

1 Corinthians 15:58

I am made a partaker of Christ, if I hold the beginning of my confidence steadfast until the end.

Hebrews 3:14

Lord GOD, You will help me, therefore I will not be disgraced; I have set my face like a flint, and I know that I shall not be ashamed.

Isaiah 50:7

I am strong; and I do not let my hands become weak, for my work shall be rewarded.

2 Chronicles 15:7

PERSEVERANCE

Save me, O God, by Your name, and judge me by Your
strength. Hear my prayer, O God; give ear to the words
of my mouth. Strangers have risen up against me, and
oppressors seek after my soul. They have not set You
before them. Behold, You are my helper. You are with
those who uphold my soul.

Psalm 54:1-4

I am troubled on every side, yet not distressed; I am
perplexed, but not in despair; persecuted, but not
forsaken; cast down, but not destroyed; always bearing
about in my body the dying of the Lord Jesus, that the
life also of Jesus might be made manifest in my body.
For I who live am always delivered to death for Jesus'
sake, that the life also of Jesus might be made manifest
in my mortal flesh.

2 Corinthians 4:8-11

Nothing great was ever done without much enduring.
Catherine of Siena

PRAYER

*"B*uilding yourselves up on your most holy faith,
praying in the Holy Spirit, keep yourselves in My love."

Jude 20-21

The effectual fervent prayer of the righteous avails
much.

James 5:16

I exhort therefore, that, first of all, supplications,
prayers, intercessions, and giving of thanks, be made for
all men, for kings [government leaders], and for all who
are in authority, that we may lead a quiet and peaceable
life in all godliness and honesty. For this is good and
acceptable in the sight of God our Savior, who will have
all people to be saved, and to come to the knowledge
of the truth.

1 Timothy 2:1-4

Your eyes, Lord, are over the righteous, and Your ears
are open to their prayers.

1 Peter 3:12

"The end of all things is at hand, be therefore sober,
and watch for the purpose of prayer."

1 Peter 4:7

PRAYER

"Be anxious for nothing, but in everything by prayer and supplication with thanksgiving, let your requests be made known to Me. And My peace, which passes all understanding, shall keep your hearts and minds through Christ Jesus."

Philippians 4:6-7

The Spirit also helps my infirmities, for I do not know what I should pray for as I ought, but the Spirit Himself makes intercession for us with groanings, which cannot be uttered. He who searches the hearts knows what is the mind of the Spirit, because He makes intercession for the saints according to Your will, God.

Romans 8:26-27

[Paul wrote:] "We are ambassadors for Christ, as though God did beseech you by us, we pray for you in Christ's stead, be reconciled to God. For He has made Him to be sin for us, who knew no sin, that we might be made the righteousness of God in Him."

2 Corinthians 5:20-21

Prayer

The prayer of faith shall save the sick, and You, Lord,
shall raise him up.

James 5:15

"Know that I have set apart the one who is godly for
themselves: I, your LORD will hear when you call
to Me."

Psalm 4:3

LORD, You have heard the desire of the humble:
thou wilt prepare their heart, thou wilt cause thine ear
to hear.

Psalm 10:17

Pray for us, that the word of the Lord may have free
course, and be glorified, even as it is with you, and that
we may be delivered from unreasonable and wicked
men, for not all men have faith. But the Lord is
faithful, who shall establish you and keep you from evil.

2 Thessalonians 3:1-3

There is nothing that makes us love
a man so much as praying for him.

William Law

SELF-CONTROL

"*K*eep your heart with all diligence, for out of it flow the issues of life."

Proverbs 4:23

Out of the abundance of the heart my mouth speaks. A good man out of the good treasure of the heart brings forth good things. An evil man brings evil things out of an evil treasure. . . . By my words I shall be justified, and by my words I shall be condemned.

Matthew 12:34-35,37

"You shall be hated by all men for My name's sake, but not a hair of your head will perish. In your patience, possess your souls."

Luke 21:17-19

"Better is the end of a thing than the beginning of it, and the patient in spirit is better than the proud in spirit. Be not hasty in your spirit to become angry, for anger rests in the bosom of fools."

Ecclesiastes 7:8-9

Self-control

I, who am slow to get angry, am of great understanding.
But the one who is hasty of spirit exalts folly.

Proverbs 14:29

The fruit of Your Spirit is love, joy, peace, longsuffering,
gentleness, goodness, faith, meekness, temperance.
There is no law against these things.

Galatians 5:22-23

"Let everyone be swift to hear, slow to speak, slow
to get angry, for the anger of person does not work
My righteousness."

James 1:19-20

Whoever keeps his mouth and his tongue, keeps his
soul from troubles.

Proverbs 21:23

I will take heed to my ways so that I do not sin with my
tongue. I will keep my mouth as with a bridle while the
wicked is before me.

Psalm 39:1

Even a fool when he keeps his mouth shut, is considered wise. I who shut my lips am esteemed as a person
of understanding.

Proverbs 17:28

SELF-CONTROL

I, who am Christ's, have crucified the flesh with affections and lusts. If I live in the Spirit, let me also walk in the Spirit.

Galatians 5:24-25

If I live after the flesh, I shall die. But if, through the Spirit, I kill the deeds of the body, I shall live.

Romans 8:13

You are a God ready to pardon, gracious and merciful, slow to anger, and very kind. You did not forsake me.

Nehemiah 9:17

Herein is my love made perfect so that I may have boldness in the day of judgment, because as You are, so am I in this world.

1 John 4:17

The one who is void of wisdom despises his neighbor, but a person of understanding holds their peace.

Proverbs 11:12

Lord of himself, though not of lands;
And having nothing, yet hath all.

Sir Henry Wotton

STRENGTH

LORD, You are my strength and my shield; my heart trusted in You, and I am helped. Therefore, my heart greatly rejoices and with my song will I praise You. You, LORD, are my strength and You are the saving strength of Your anointed.

Psalm 28:7-8

You, LORD, are my strength and song, and are become my salvation.

Psalm 118:14

"My grace is sufficient for you, for My strength is made perfect in weakness." Most gladly, then, I will rather glory in my infirmities that the power of Christ may rest upon me. . . . For when I am weak, then I am strong.

2 Corinthians 12:9-10

LORD, Your way is strength to the upright, but destruction will come upon the workers of wrongdoing.

Proverbs 10:29

STRENGTH

I know that You, LORD, save Your anointed. You will hear him from Your holy heaven with the saving strength of Your right hand. Some people trust in chariots and some in horses, but I will remember Your name, LORD my God.

Psalm 20:6-7

To You, O my strength, will I sing, for You, God, are my defense and the God of my mercy.

Psalm 59:17

God, You are my strength and power, and You make my way blameless.

2 Samuel 22:33

"Be strong in Me, your LORD, and in the power of My might. Put on My whole armor, so that you may be able to stand against the wiles of the devil."

Ephesians 6:10-11

Let the words of my mouth and the meditation of my heart be acceptable in Your sight, O LORD, my strength and my redeemer.

Psalm 19:14

STRENGTH

The salvation of the righteous is of You, LORD. You are my strength in times of trouble.

Psalm 37:39

"Be strong and of good courage. . . . And the LORD—I, who do go before you—I will be with you. I will not fail you nor forsake you. Fear not, neither be dismayed."

Deuteronomy 31:7-8

You have girded me with strength for battle. You subdued under me those who rose up against me.

2 Samuel 22:40

Both riches and honor come from You, and You reign over all. In Your hand is power and might; and it is in Your hand to make great and to give strength to all [even me].

1 Chronicles 29:12

LORD God, You are my strength, and You will make my feet like deer's feet. You will make me to walk upon my high places.

Habakkuk 3:19

STRENGTH

God, Your weakness is stronger than men.

1 Corinthians 1:25

Be sober and vigilant, because your adversary the devil walks around like a roaring lion, seeking whom he may devour. Steadfastly resist him in the faith, knowing that the same afflictions are happening to your fellow believers who are in the world.

1 Peter 5:8-9

Have I not commanded you? Be strong and of good courage. Do not be afraid nor be dismayed, for the LORD your God is with you wherever you go.

Joshua 1:9

LORD, You will give strength to Your people; You, LORD, will bless Your people with peace.

Psalm 29:11

Trust in the LORD, forever, for in the LORD JEHOVAH is everlasting strength.

Isaiah 26:4

Your eyes, LORD, run to and fro throughout the whole earth, to show Yourself strong in the behalf of those whose heart is perfect toward You.

2 Chronicles 16:9

STRENGTH

LORD, bow down Your ear to me; deliver me speedily;
be my strong rock, for a house of defense to save me.
For You are my rock and my fortress; therefore for Your
name's sake lead me and guide me.

Psalm 31:2-3

Glory and honor are in Your presence; strength and
gladness are in Your place.

1 Chronicles 16:27

[Israel] did not get the land in possession by their own
sword, and neither did their own arm save them, but
Your right hand and Your arm and the light of Your
countenance, because You favored them. . . . Through
You I will push down my enemies; through Your name
I will tread over those who rise up against me.

Psalm 44:3,5

So let it be in God's own might
We gird us for the coming fight,
And, strong in him whose cause is ours,
In conflict with unholy powers,
We grasp the weapons he has given,
The light and truth and love of heaven.

John Greenleaf Whittier

SUCCESS

"*T*his book of the law shall not depart out of your mouth, but you shall meditate in it day and night, that you may observe to do according to all that is written in it, for then you shall make your way prosperous, and then you shall have good success."

Joshua 1:8

"It shall come to pass, if you shall hearken diligently to the voice of the LORD your God, to observe and to do all His commandments which I command you this day, that I, the LORD your God, will set you on high above all nations of the earth. And all these blessings shall come on you and overtake you, if you shall hearken to the voice of the LORD your God. . . . The LORD shall command the blessing upon you in your store-houses, and in all that you set your hand to."

Deuteronomy 28:1-2,8

The slothful person roasts not that which they took in hunting, but the substance of the diligent person is precious.

Proverbs 12:27

SUCCESS

He becomes poor that deals with a slack hand, but the hand of the diligent makes rich.

Proverbs 10:4

The hand of the diligent shall bear rule, but the slothful shall be under tribute.

Proverbs 12:24

"Because you have set your love upon Me, therefore will I deliver you. I will set you on high, because you have known My name."

Psalm 91:14

It is good and proper for one to eat and to drink, and to enjoy the good of all his labor that they take under the sun all the days of their life, which You, God, give them. For it is their portion. Every person also to whom You have given riches and wealth, and have given them power to eat of it, and to take their portion, and to rejoice in their labor, this is Your gift, God.

Ecclesiastes 5:18-19

SUCCESS

Blessed is the one who does not walk in the counsel of the ungodly, nor stands in the way of sinners, nor sits in the seat of the scornful. But their delight is in Your law, LORD, and in Your law do they meditate day and night. And they shall be like a tree planted by the rivers of water, that bring forth their fruit in their season. Their leaf also shall not wither, and whatever they do shall prosper.

Psalm 1:1-3

Promotion comes neither from the east, nor from the west, nor from the south. But You, God, are the judge. You put down one, and set up another.

Psalm 75:5

Who aimeth at the sky
Shoots higher much than he that means a tree.

George Herbert

THANKSGIVING

*F*irst of all, I make supplications, prayers, intercessions, and give thanks for all men, for kings and for all that are in authority so that I may lead a quiet and peaceable life in all godliness and honesty.

1 Timothy 2:1-2

Every one of Your creatures is good, and none of them is to be refused [as food], if I receive it with thanksgiving, for it is sanctified by Your word and prayer.

1 Timothy 4:4-5

I give thanks to You, Father, for You have qualified me to partake of the inheritance of the saints in light.

Colossians 1:12

I come before Your presence with thanksgiving and make a joyful sound to You with psalms. For You, LORD, are a great God and a great King above all gods.

Psalm 95:2-3

I give thanks to You, LORD, for You are good and Your mercy endures forever.

1 Chronicles 16:34

THANKSGIVING

By Jesus I continually offer the sacrifice of praise to
You, God, that is the fruit of my lips giving thanks
to Your name.

Hebrews 13:15

In everything I give You thanks, God, for this is Your
will concerning me in Christ Jesus.

1 Thessalonians 5:18

All Your works shall praise You, O LORD, and I shall
bless You. I shall speak of the glory of Your kingdom
and talk of Your power.

Psalm 145:10-11

For each new morning with its light,
Father, we thank thee,
For rest and shelter of the night,
Father, we thank thee,
For health and food, for love and friends,
For everything thy goodness sends,
Father, in heaven, we thank thee.

Ralph Waldo Emerson

A CHRIST-LIKE HEART REFLECTS GOD'S . . .
UNDERSTANDING

$\mathcal{G}$od, You make me a person that has understanding
of the times, to know what I ought to do.

1 Chronicles 12:32

The fear of You, LORD, is the beginning of wisdom. I
have a good understanding because I do Your
commandments. Your praise endures forever.

Psalm 111:10

There is no wisdom nor understanding nor counsel that
is against You, LORD.

Proverbs 21:30

"Incline your ear and come to Me, hear and your soul
shall live. . . . My thoughts are not your thoughts,
neither are your ways My ways. For as the heavens are
higher than the earth, so are My ways higher than your
ways and My thoughts than your thoughts."

Isaiah 55:3,8-9

God, You are King of all the earth. I sing Your praises
with understanding.

Psalm 47:7

Understanding

The one who refuses instruction despises their
own soul, but the one who listens to reprimands
gains understanding.

Proverbs 15:32

I have more understanding than all my teachers, for
Your testimonies are my meditation.

Psalm 119:99

Counsel in the human heart is like deep water, but I am
a person of understanding and draw it out.

Proverbs 20:5

Through Your precepts I get understanding, therefore I
hate every false way.

Psalm 119:104

The entrance of Your words gives light; it gives
understanding to the simple.

Psalm 119:130

How much better is it to get wisdom than gold! And
to get understanding is better than to choose silver!

Proverbs 16:16

Understanding

God, I know that Your Son has come and has given me understanding so that I may know Him who is true. I am in Him who is true.

1 John 5:20

Discretion will preserve me, and understanding will keep me. They will deliver me from the way of the evil man.

Proverbs 2:11-12

I forsake the foolish and live. I go in the way of understanding.

Proverbs 9:6

Good understanding gives me favor, but the way of sinners is hard.

Proverbs 13:15

Understanding is a fountain of life to the one who has it, but the instruction of fools is nonsense.

Proverbs 16:22

LORD, give me understanding and I shall keep Your law. Yes, I will observe it with my whole heart.

Psalm 119:34

UNDERSTANDING

The heart of the one who has understanding seeks
knowledge, but the mouth of fools feeds on foolishness.

Proverbs 15:14

The one who shuts his lips is esteemed a person
of understanding.

Proverbs 17:28

The one who gets wisdom loves their own soul. The
one who keeps understanding shall find good.

Proverbs 19:8

Give me, Your servant, an understanding heart . . . that
I may discern between good and bad.

1 Kings 3:9

If there is anything hidden from us as disciples today,
it is because we are not in a fit state to understand it.
As soon as we become fit in spiritual character,
the thing is revealed. It is concealed at God's
discretion until the life is developed sufficiently.

Oswald Chambers

VISION

*Y*our counsel, LORD, stands forever, the thoughts of
Your heart to all generations.

Psalm 33:11

Surely, Lord GOD, You will do nothing, but You reveal
Your secret to Your servants the prophets.

Amos 3:7

The LORD answered me, and said, "Write the vision,
and make it plain upon tables, that the one may run
who reads it. For the vision is yet for an appointed
time, but at the end it shall speak, and not lie. Though
it tarry, I wait for it, because it will surely come, it will
not tarry."

Habakkuk 2:2-3

"Call to Me, and I will answer you, and show you great
and mighty things, which you do not know."

Jeremiah 33:3

"'I know the thoughts I think toward you,' says the
LORD, 'thoughts of peace, and not of evil, to give you
an expected end.'"

Jeremiah 29:11

VISION

God, You reveal the deep and secret things. You know what is in the darkness, and the light dwells with You.

Daniel 2:22

Eye has not seen, nor ear heard, neither has entered into the heart of man, the things which You, God, have prepared for those who love You. But You have revealed them to us by Your Spirit, for the Spirit searches all things, yes, Your deep things, God.

1 Corinthians 2:9-10

"'It shall come to pass in the last days,' says God, 'I will pour out of My Spirit upon all flesh, and your sons and your daughters shall prophesy, and your young men shall see visions, and your old men shall dream dreams. And on My servants and on My handmaidens I will pour out in those days of My Spirit, and they shall prophesy.'"

Acts 2:17-18

"Waiting upon God is necessary in order to see Him, to have a vision of Him. . . . Our hearts are like a sensitive photographer's plate; and in order to have God revealed there, we must sit at His feet a long time."—Dr. Pardington

Lettie B. Cowman

WISDOM

*T*he wise in heart will receive commandments, but a chattering fool shall fall.

Proverbs 10:8

I will not be wise in my own eyes. I fear You, LORD, and I depart from evil. This will be health to my body and refreshment to my bones.

Proverbs 3:7-8

Through wisdom is my house built, and by understanding it is established. By knowledge shall the rooms be filled with all precious and pleasant riches.

Proverbs 24:3-4

I will give you an open mouth and wisdom, which all your adversaries shall not be able to contradict nor resist.

Luke 21:15

In Christ are hidden all the treasures of wisdom and knowledge.

Colossians 2:3

God, You made Christ wisdom, righteousness, sanctification, and redemption to me.

1 Corinthians 1:30

WISDOM

LORD, as Your child, I do not despise Your discipline and I am not weary of Your correction, for You correct those whom You love, LORD, as a father corrects the child he delights in.

Proverbs 3:11-12

Wisdom dwells with good sense, and finds knowledge and discretion.

Proverbs 8:12

The wisdom that You give me is from above. It is first pure, then peaceable, gentle, and easily persuaded, full of mercy and good fruits, impartial, and without hypocrisy.

James 3:17

LORD, You give me wisdom. Out of Your mouth comes knowledge and understanding. You lay up sound wisdom for me who has been made righteous.

Proverbs 2:6-7

Through Your commandments, You have made me wiser than my enemies.

Psalm 119:98

By wisdom my days will be multiplied and the years of my life will be increased.

Proverbs 9:11

I have the mind of Christ.

1 Corinthians 2:16

WISDOM

If I lack wisdom, God, I ask You for it. You give
wisdom liberally to me, and You do not reprimand
me for asking.

James 1:5

Wisdom is more precious than rubies, and all the things
I can desire cannot be compared to her. Long life is in
her right hand, and in her left hand are riches and
honor. Her ways are pleasant, and all her paths are
peaceful. She is a tree of life to me as I lay hold of her,
and I am happy because I hold on to her.

Proverbs 3:15-18

The tongue of the wise is health.

Proverbs 12:18

Christ has lavished Your grace on me with all wisdom
and good sense.

Ephesians 1:8-9

I will bless You, LORD, who have given me counsel.
My innermost being also instructs me in the nighttime.

Psalm 16:7

WISDOM

The words of the wise are heard in quiet more than the cry of the one who rules among fools.

Ecclesiastes 9:17

I have an anointing from the Holy One, and I know the truth.

1 John 2:20

O LORD, how diverse are Your works! In wisdom You have made everything. The earth is full of Your riches.

Psalm 104:24

LORD, by wisdom You have founded the earth; by understanding You have established the heavens.

Proverbs 3:19

I commit my works to You, LORD, and my thoughts will be established.

Proverbs 16:3

Wisdom and knowledge will be the stability of my times and the strength of my salvation.

Isaiah 33:6

Wisdom

Wisdom loves me who loves her; and I seek her early
and find her.

Proverbs 8:17

When I hear Jesus' sayings and do them, I am like a
wise man who built his house upon a rock.

Matthew 7:24

Your foolishness, God, is wiser than the wisdom
of men.

1 Corinthians 1:25

The holy Scriptures are able to make me wise for my
salvation through faith which is in Christ Jesus.

2 Timothy 3:15

I am happy when I find wisdom and get understanding,
for the profit from it is better than the profit from
silver, and what I gain from it is more profitable than
the gain from fine gold.

Proverbs 3:13-14

*May we not ask Him to bring His perfect foreknowledge
to bear on all our mental training and storing? To guide
us to read or study exactly what He knows there will be
use for in the work to which He has called or will call us?*

Frances Ridley Havergal

ZEAL

*T*he effectual fervent prayer of a righteous person
avails much.

James 5:16

Your grace, God, that brings salvation has appeared to
all people, teaching us that, denying ungodliness and
worldly lusts, we should live soberly, righteously, and
godly, in this present world, looking for that blessed
hope, and the glorious appearing of the great God and
our Savior Jesus Christ, who gave Himself for us, that
He might redeem us from all wrongdoing, and purify to
Himself a peculiar people, zealous of good works.

Titus 2:11-14

Seeing you have purified your souls in obeying the truth
through the Spirit to sincere love of the believers, see
that you love one another with a pure heart fervently,
being born again, not of corruptible seed, but incorrupt-
ible, by the word of God, which lives and abides forever.

1 Peter 1:22-23

ZEAL

It is good to be zealously affected always in a
good thing.

Galatians 4:18

My zeal has consumed me, because my enemies have
forgotten Your words. Your word is very pure, therefore
your servant loves it.

Psalm 119:139-140

"Above all things have fervent love among yourselves,
for love shall cover the multitude of sins."

1 Peter 4:8

"Whatever your hand finds to do, do it with your
might, for there is no work, nor device, nor knowledge,
nor wisdom, in the grave."

Ecclesiastes 9:10

To us a Child is born, to us a Son is given, and the
government shall be upon His shoulder, and His name
shall be called Wonderful, Counselor, The mighty God,
The everlasting Father, The Prince of Peace. Of the
increase of His government and peace there shall be
no end. . . . Your zeal, LORD of hosts, will perform this.

Isaiah 9:6-7

ZEAL

My heart's desire and prayer to God for Israel is, that they might be saved. For I bear them record that they have a zeal of God, but not according to knowledge. For they, being ignorant of God's righteousness and going about to establish their own righteousness, have not submitted themselves to the righteousness of God. For Christ is the end of the law for righteousness to everyone who believes.

Romans 10:1-4

As many as I love, I rebuke and chasten. Be zealous therefore, and repent.

Revelation 3:19

Spirit-filled souls are ablaze for God. They love with a love that glows. They believe with a faith that kindles. They serve with a devotion that consumes. They hate sin with a fierceness that burns. They rejoice with a joy that radiates. Love is perfected in the fire of God.

Samuel Chadwick

A GRADUATE
RELIES ON GOD
REGARDING . . .

*T*he ones who have taken a stand, who have drawn a boundary-line sharp and deep about their religious life, who have marked off all beyond as forever forbidden ground to them, find the yoke easy and the burden light. For this forbidden environment comes to be as if it were not. . . . And the balm of death numbing the lower nature releases them for the scarce disturbed communion of a higher life. So even here to die is gain.

Henry Drummond

Since we have so great a cloud of witnesses surrounding us, let us also lay aside every encumbrance, and the sin which so easily entangles us, and let us run with endurance the race that is set before us.

Hebrews 12:1 NASB

ANGER

A wise man fears and departs from evil, but the fool rages and is reckless. The one who is quickly angered deals foolishly. . . . The one who is slow to anger is of great understanding, but the one who is quick-tempered exalts stupidity.

Proverbs 14:16-17,29

"Love your enemies, bless those who curse you, do good to those who hate you, and pray for those who despitefully use you, and persecute you, that you may be the children of your Father who is in heaven. For I make My sun to rise on the evil and on the good, and send rain on the just and on the unjust."

Matthew 5:44-45

Let everyone be quick to hear, slow to speak, and slow to anger, for the human anger does not produce Your righteousness, God.

James 1:19-20

ANGER

A soft answer turns away anger. But harsh words stir up anger. . . . A furious man stirs up strife, but the one who is slow to anger calms strife.

Proverbs 15:1,18

"Do all things without grumbling and debating so that you may be blameless and innocent, My children who are without rebuke, in the midst of a crooked and perverted nation, among whom you shine as a light in the world."

Philippians 2:14-15

The discretion of a person defers their anger, and it is to their glory to pass over a transgression.

Proverbs 19:11

The one who is slow to anger is better than the mighty; and the one who rules their spirit than one who captures a city.

Proverbs 16:32

The one who despises their neighbor sins; but the one who has mercy on the poor, this person is happy.

Proverbs 14:21

ANGER

Wise people turn away wrath.

Proverbs 29:8

[Paul wrote:] "Put away lying, speak truth with your neighbor, for we are members of one another. Be angry but do not sin. Do not let the sun go down on your wrath."

Ephesians 4:25-26

[Paul wrote:] All the law is fulfilled in one word, even in this: "You shall love your neighbor as yourself. But if you bite and devour one another, take heed that you do not consume one another." This I say then, "Walk in the Spirit, and you will not fulfill the lust of the flesh."

Galatians 5:14-16

"Put off all these: anger, wrath, malice . . . seeing that you have put off the old man with his deeds and have put on the new man which is renewed in knowledge after the image of Me, the one who created you."

Colossians 3:8,10

Anger is a weed, hate is the tree.

Augustine of Hippo

ANXIETY

*C*ause me to hear Your lovingkindness in the morning,
for in You do I trust. Cause me to know the way in
which I should walk; for I lift up my soul to You. . . .
Teach me to do Your will, for You are my God. Your
Spirit is good. Lead me into the land of uprightness. . . .
For Your righteousness' sake bring my soul out
of trouble.

Psalm 143:8,10-11

It is vain for me to rise up early, to sit up late, to eat the
bread of sorrows, for You give Your beloved sleep.

Psalm 127:2

I have trusted also in You, LORD; therefore I shall
not slide.

Psalm 26:1

Casting all my care upon You, for You care for me.

1 Peter 5:7

When I said, My foot slips, Your mercy, O LORD,
held me up.

Psalm 94:18

ANXIETY

Surely I shall not be moved forever. The righteous shall be in everlasting remembrance. I shall not be afraid of evil tidings. My heart is fixed, trusting in You, LORD.

Psalm 112:6-7

Show Your marvelous lovingkindness, O You who save by Your right hand those who put their trust in You from those who rise up against them. Keep me as the apple of the eye, hide me under the shadow of Your wings.

Psalm 17:7-8

I have set you, LORD, always before me, because You are at my right hand, I shall not be moved. Therefore my heart is glad, and my glory rejoices. My flesh also shall rest in hope.

Psalm 16:8-9

I will both lay myself down in peace, and sleep, for You, LORD, only make me dwell in safety.

Psalm 4:7

God never built a Christian strong enough to carry today's duties and tomorrow's anxieties piled on top of them..

Theodore Ledyard Cuyler

ATTITUDE

"Let this mind be in you, which was also in Christ Jesus, who, being in My form, thought it not robbery to be equal with Me, but made Himself of no reputation, and took upon Himself the form of a servant, and was made in the likeness of men. And being found in fashion as a man, He humbled Himself, and became obedient to death, even the death of the cross. For this I also have highly exalted Him, and given Him a name which is above every name."

Philippians 2:5-9

[The man] answering said, "You shall love the Lord your God with all your heart, and with all your soul, and with all your strength, and with all your mind, and your neighbor as yourself." And [Jesus] said to him, . . ."Do this and you shall live."

Luke 10:27-28

ATTITUDE

"Be renewed in the spirit of your mind, and put on the new man, which after Me is created in righteousness and true holiness."

Ephesians 4:23-24

"Put on therefore, as My elect, holy and beloved, a merciful heart, kindness, humility, meekness, longsuffering, forbearing one another, and forgiving one another, if anyone has a quarrel against any; even as Christ forgave you, so also do you. And above all these things put on love, which is the perfect bond of unity."

Colossians 3:12-14

"Whatever your hand finds to do, do it with your might, for there is no work, nor device, nor knowledge, nor wisdom, in the grave, where you will go."

Ecclesiastes 9:10

"Do all things without murmurings and disputings, that you may be blameless and harmless, My children, without rebuke, in the midst of a crooked and perverse nation, among whom you shine as lights in the world."

Philippians 2:14-15

ATTITUDE

"Gird up the loins of your mind, be sober, and hope to the end for the grace that is to be brought to you at the revelation of Jesus Christ, as obedient children, not fashioning yourselves according to the former lusts in your ignorance. But as I who have called you am holy, so you be holy in all manner of life, because it is written, 'Be holy, for I am holy.'"

1 Peter 1:13-16

"All of you be of one mind, having compassion one for another, love one another, be sympathetic, be courteous, not repaying evil for evil, or abuse for abuse, but on the contrary blessing, knowing that you are called to this, that you should inherit a blessing."

1 Peter 3:8-9

Who has known the mind of the Lord, so as to instruct Him? But I have the mind of Christ.

1 Corinthians 2:16

ATTITUDE

[David wrote:] "Serve the LORD with gladness. Come before His presence with singing. Know that the LORD is God. It is He who has made us, and not we ourselves. We are His people, and the sheep of His pasture. Enter into His gates with thanksgiving, and into His courts with praise. Be thankful to Him, and bless His name. For He is good; His mercy is everlasting, and His truth endures to all generations."

Psalm 100:2-5

[Paul wrote:] "Rejoice in the Lord always, and again I say, 'Rejoice.' Let your moderation be known to all. The Lord is at hand."

Philippians 4:4-5

"I have set before you life and death, blessing and cursing; therefore choose life, that both you and your seed may live."

Deuteronomy 30:19

Doubt indulged soon becomes doubt realized.
Frances Ridley Havergal

CONFLICT

[*P*aul wrote:] "We do not wrestle against flesh and
blood, but against principalities, against powers, against
the rulers of the darkness of this world, against spiritual
wickedness in high places. Wherefore take the whole
armor of God, that you may be able to withstand in
the evil day."

Ephesians 6:12

Christ also suffered for me, leaving me an example,
that I should follow His steps. . . . When He was
insulted, He did not insult in reply; when He suffered,
He did not threaten but committed Himself to You
who judges righteously.

1 Peter 2:21,23

You shall hide me in the secret of Your presence
from the snares of man. You shall keep me secretly in
a pavilion from the strife of tongues.

Psalm 31:20

Cast out the scoffer and contention will go out; yes,
strife and shame shall cease.

Proverbs 22:10

Conflict

Many are the afflictions of the righteous, but You,
LORD, deliver him out of them all.

Psalm 34:19

Where no wood is, the fire goes out. Similarly, where
there is no talebearer, the strife ceases.

Proverbs 26:20

The one who is of a proud heart, stirs up strife; but the
one who puts his trust in You, LORD, shall be satisfied.

Proverbs 28:25

"When you stand praying, forgive, if you have anything
against anyone so that I, your Father who is in heaven,
may forgive you your offenses. But if you do not forgive,
neither will I forgive you for your offenses."

Mark 11:25-26

"Be complete, be of good comfort, be of one mind,
live in peace; and, I, the God of love and peace, will be
with you."

2 Corinthians 13:11

When someone's ways please You, LORD, You make
even their enemies to be at peace with them.

Proverbs 16:7

CONFLICT

It is an honor for me to cease from strife, but every fool will be meddling.

Proverbs 20:3

I, who love my brother, dwell in the light; and there is no occasion of stumbling in me. But the one who hates his brother is in darkness and walks in darkness and doesn't know where he is going, because that darkness has blinded his eyes.

1 John 2:10-11

"Pursue peace with all people, and holiness, without which you shall not see Me, your Lord."

Hebrews 12:14

I will cry to You, God most high, to You who perform all things for me. You shall send from heaven and save me from the reproach of the one who would swallow me up. You shall send forth Your mercy and Your truth.

Psalm 57:2-3

Would not the carrying out of one single commandment of Christ, "Love one another," change the whole aspect of the world and sweep away prisons and workhouses, and envying and strife, and all the strongholds of the devil?

Max Muller

CONFUSION

*G*od, You are not the author of confusion, but of peace.

1 Corinthians 14:33

"Let My peace rule in your hearts, to which also you are called in one body, and be thankful."

Colossians 3:15

Where envying and strife is, there is confusion and every evil work. But the wisdom that is from above is first pure, then peaceable, gentle, and easy to be entreated, full of mercy and good fruits, without partiality, and without hypocrisy.

James 3:16-17

[Jesus said:] "My sheep hear My voice, and I call his own sheep by name, and lead them out. And when I puts forth My own sheep, I go before them, and the sheep follow Me, for they know My voice. And a stranger they will not follow, but will flee from him, for they do not know the voice of strangers."

John 10:3-5

Confusion

"Everyone who is of the truth hears My voice."

John 18:37

Your word is a lamp to my feet, and a light to my path.

Psalm 119:105

Cause me to hear Your lovingkindess in the morning;
for in You do I trust. Cause me to know the way in
which I should walk, for I lift up my soul to You.

Psalm 143:8

Lead me, O LORD, in Your righteousness because of
my enemies. Make Your way straight before my face.

Psalm 5:8

In You, O LORD, do I put my trust. Never let me be
put to confusion. Deliver me in Your righteousness, and
cause me to escape. Incline Your ear to me, and save
me. Be my strong habitation, where I may continually
resort. You have given commandment to save me, for
You are my rock and my fortress.

Psalm 71:1-3

CONFUSION

"I will bring the blind by a way that they did not know,
I will lead them in paths that they have not known.
I will make darkness light before them, and crooked
things straight. These things will I do to them, and
not forsake them."

Isaiah 42:16

"If any of you lack wisdom, ask of Me, who gives to
all liberally, and does not reprimand you for asking,
and it shall be given to you. But ask in faith, with no
wavering. For the one who wavers is like a wave of
the sea driven with the wind and tossed . . . A double
minded person is unstable in all ways."

James 1:5-6,8

"Be still, and know that I am God."

Psalm 46:10

Without God, the world would be a maze without a clue.
Woodrow Wilson

DEPRESSION

$\mathcal{T}$he sorrows of death surround me. . . . The sorrows
of hell surround me on every side; the noose of death
goes before me. In my distress I called upon You,
LORD, and cried to You, my God. You heard my voice
out of Your temple, and my cry came before You into
Your ears. . . . You sent from above, You took me and
drew me out of many waters.

Psalm 18:4-6,16

You, LORD, preserve the simple. I was brought low, and
You helped me. Return to your rest, O my soul; for the
LORD has dealt bountifully with you. For You, LORD,
have delivered my soul from death, my eyes from tears,
and my feet from falling.

Psalm 116:6-8

LORD, You will be a refuge to the oppressed, a refuge
in times of trouble.

Psalm 9:9

DEPRESSION

You deliver me in my affliction when I am poor and
open my ears in oppressions.

Job 36:15

How long shall I take counsel in my soul, having sorrow
in my heart daily? . . . Consider and hear me, O LORD
my God. Lighten my eyes, lest I sleep the sleep of
death. . . . But I have trusted in Your mercy; my heart
shall rejoice in Your salvation.

Psalm 13:2-3,5

LORD, You will give me rest from my sorrow, and from
my fear, and from the hard bondage in which I was
made to serve.

Isaiah 14:3

You satisfy my longing soul and fill my hungry soul
with goodness.

Psalm 107:9

God, You anointed Jesus of Nazareth with the Holy
Spirit and with power, who went about doing good and
healing all who were oppressed of the devil, for You
were with Him.

Acts 10:38

DEPRESSION

I will be glad and rejoice in Your mercy, for You
have considered my trouble; You have known my soul
in adversities.

Psalm 31:7

You will fulfill the desire of those who fear You. You
also will hear their cry and will save them. You, LORD,
preserve all who love You.

Psalm 145:19-20

O LORD, You have brought up my soul from the grave.
You have kept me alive that I should not go down to
the pit.

Psalm 30:3

Your anger endures but a moment; in Your favor is life.
Weeping may endure for a night, but joy comes in
the morning.

Psalm 30:5

LORD, You execute judgment for me when I am
oppressed. You give food to me when I am hungry.
LORD, You loose me when I am prisoner. You open
my eyes when they are blind. You raise me when I am
bowed down. You love the righteous.

Psalm 146:7-8

DEPRESSION

My heart is sore pained within me, and the terrors of
death are fallen upon me. Fearfulness and trembling are
come upon me, and horror has overwhelmed me. As for
me, I will call upon You, God, and You shall save me.
Evening, and morning, and at noon, will I pray and cry
aloud; and You shall hear my voice.

Psalm 55:4-5,16-17

Do not let the flood overflow me, neither let the deep
swallow me up, and do not let the pit shut her mouth
upon me. Hear me, O LORD, for Your loving kindness
is good. Turn to me according to the multitude of
Your tender mercies. And hide not Your face from Your
servant, for I am in trouble. Hear me speedily.

Psalm 69:15-17

When I cried to You, the LORD God of my fathers,
You heard my voice and looked on my affliction, and
my labor, and my oppression.

Deuteronomy 26:7

DEPRESSION

O God, You are my God; I will seek You early. My
soul thirsts for You, my flesh longs for You in a dry and
thirsty land, where no water is. . . . Because You have
been my help, therefore in the shadow of Your wings
I will rejoice.

Psalm 63:1,7-8

As the deer pants after the water brooks, so pants my
soul after You, O God. My soul thirsts for You, for the
living God. When shall I come and appear before You?
My tears have been my meat day and night, while they
continually say to me, "Where is your God?" . . . Deep
calls to deep at the noise of your waterspouts. All Your
waves and Your billows are gone over me. Yet You,
LORD, will command Your lovingkindness in the
daytime, and in the night Your song shall be with me,
and my prayer to You, the God of my life.

Psalm 42:1-4,7-8

DEPRESSION

My offenses have gone over my head, as a heavy
burden, they are too heavy for me. . . . I am troubled;
I am bowed down greatly; I go mourning all; the day
long. . . . My heart pants, my strength fails me. As for
the light of my eyes, it also is gone from me. . . . In
You, O LORD, do I hope. You will hear, O Lord my
God. . . . Do not forsake me, LORD. O my God, do
not be far from me. Make haste to help me, O Lord
of my salvation.

Psalm 38:4,6,10,15,21-22

The dayspring from on high has visited me, to give me
light who sits in darkness and in the shadow of death,
to guide my feet into the way of peace.

Luke 1:78-79

Lead, kindly Light, amid th' encircling gloom;
Lead thou me on.
The night is dark, and I am far from home;
Lead thou me on.
Keep thou my feet; I do not ask to see
The distant scene—one step enough for me.

Cardinal John Henry Newman

DISCOURAGEMENT

LORD, You lead me beside still waters. You restore
my soul.

Psalm 23:2-3

"Repent and be converted, that your sins may be blotted
out, when the times of refreshing shall come from the
presence of your Lord."

Acts 3:19

Let me not be weary in well doing, for in due season I
shall reap, if I faint not.

Galatians 6:9

If I give out my soul to the hungry and satisfy the
afflicted soul, then will my light rise in obscurity and
my darkness will be as the noonday. You, LORD, will
guide me continually and satisfy my soul in drought and
strengthen my bones. I shall be like a watered garden
and like a spring of water, whose waters do not fail.

Isaiah 58:10-11

You keep track of my wanderings. You put my tears into
Your bottle. Are they not in Your book?

Psalm 56:8

Discouragement

My soul is melted because of trouble. . . . I am at my wit's end. Then I cry out to You, LORD, in my trouble, and You bring me out of my distresses. You make the storm calm so that the waves are still. Then I am glad because they are quiet, and You bring me to my desired haven.

Psalm 107:26-30

My flesh and my heart fail, but You, God, are the strength of my heart and my portion forever.

Psalm 73:26

You, LORD, are good to all, and Your tender mercies are over all Your works.

Psalm 145:9

Because I have set my love upon You, You will deliver me. You will set me on high, because I have known Your name. I call on You, and You will answer me. You will be with me in trouble; You will deliver me and honor me.

Psalm 91:14-15

DISCOURAGEMENT

The hope of the righteous shall be gladness, but the
expectation of the wicked will perish.

Proverbs 10:28

Strangers have risen up against me, and oppressors seek
after my soul. They have not set You, God, before them.
Behold, You, God, are my help. You are with those who
uphold my soul.

Psalm 54:3-4

I will remember the years of Your right hand, most
High. I will remember Your works, LORD. Surely I will
remember Your wonders of old. I will meditate also on
all Your work and talk of Your doings. Your way, O
God, is in the sanctuary. Who is so great a God as our
God? You are the God who does wonders. You have
declared Your strength among the people

Psalm 77:10-14

[I am] strengthened with all might, according to
Your glorious power, to all patience and longsuffering
with joyfulness.

Colossians 1:11

Discouragement

Hear me when I call, O God of my righteousness. You have enlarged me when I was in distress. Have mercy on me, and hear my prayer.

Psalm 4:1

Happy am I who have You, the God of Jacob for my help, whose hope is in You, LORD.

Psalm 146:5

Great are Your tender mercies, O LORD. Revive me according to Your judgments.

Psalm 119:156

Whom do I have in heaven but You? There is none on the earth that I desire beside You. . . . It is good for me to draw near to You, God. I have put my trust in You so that I may declare all Your works.

Psalm 73:25,28

"Not one sparrow will fall on the ground without Me, your Father. But the very hairs on your head are all numbered; therefore, do not fear. You are of more value than many sparrows."

Matthew 10:29-30

I laid myself down and slept. I awoke, for LORD, You sustained me.

Psalm 3:5

DISCOURAGEMENT

Hope deferred makes my heart sick, but when my desire comes, it is a tree of life.

Proverbs 13:12

"Delight yourself also in Me, your LORD, and I will give you the desires of your heart."

Psalm 37:4

You have not despised nor abhorred the affliction of the afflicted; neither have You hidden Your face from them; but when they cried to You, You heard. My praise shall be of You in the great congregation.

Psalm 22:24-25

Who shall ascend into Your holy hill, LORD? Or who shall stand in Your holy place? The one who has clean hands and a pure heart, who has not lifted up his soul to vanity, nor sworn deceitfully. He shall receive the blessing from You, LORD, and righteousness from You, the God of his salvation.

Psalm 24:3-5

When we yield to discouragement, it is usually because we give too much thought to the past or to the future.

Therese of Lisieux

DOUBT

*F*aith comes by hearing, and hearing by Your word, God.

Romans 10:17

This is the confidence that I have in You, that, if I ask anything according to Your will, You hear me, and if I know that You hear me, whatever I ask, I know that I have the petitions that I desire of You.

1 John 5:14

"If you shall say to this mountain, 'Be removed, and be cast into the sea,' and shall not doubt in your heart, but shall believe that those things which you say shall come to pass, you shall have whatever you say."

Mark 11:23

Jesus said to him, "If you can believe, all things are possible to you who believes." And right away the father of the child cried out, and said with tears, "Lord, I believe; help my unbelief."

Mark 9:24-25

DOUBT

Believe in the LORD your God, so shall you be
established; believe His prophets, so shall you prosper.

2 Chronicles 20:20

"These things I have written to you who believe on the
name of the Son of God; that you may know that you
have eternal life, and that you may believe on the name
of the Son of God."

1 John 5:13

These [things] are written, that I might believe that
Jesus is the Christ, Your Son, God; and that believing I
might have life through His name.

John 20:31

"Ask in faith, nothing wavering. For the one who wavers
is like a wave of the sea driven with the wind and
tossed. For the doubter should not expect to receive
anything of the Lord. A double-minded person is
unstable in all ways."

James 1:6-8

*In times of dryness and desolation we must be patient,
and wait with resignation the return of consolation,
putting our trust in the goodness of God. We must
animate ourselves by the thought that God is always
with us, that He only allows this trial for our greater
good, and that we have not necessarily lost His grace
because we have lost the taste and feeling of it.*

Ignatius of Loyala

FEAR

A thousand shall fall at my side and ten thousand at my right hand, but it will not come near me. Only with my eyes shall I behold and see the reward of the wicked. Because I have made You, LORD, who are my refuge, even You, the most High, my habitation, no evil will befall me, neither will any plague come near my dwelling.

Psalm 91:7-10

Be of good courage and I shall strengthen your heart, all you who hope in the LORD.

Psalm 31:24

You are my hiding place and my shield. I hope in Your word. . . . Hold me up, and I shall be safe. And I will have respect for Your laws continually.

Psalm 119:114,117

FEAR

It is vain for me to rise up early, to sit up late, and eat
the bread of sorrows, for You give Your beloved sleep.

Psalm 127:2

There is no fear in love, but perfect love casts out fear,
because fear has torment.

1 John 4:18

"Thus says the LORD who created you, . . . 'Fear not,
for I have redeemed you. I have called you by your
name; you are Mine.'"

Isaiah 43:1

"Cast your burden upon Me, your LORD, and I
will sustain you. I will never allow the righteous to
be moved."

Psalm 55:22

"Peace I leave with you, My peace I give to you, not as
the world gives do I give to you. Do not let your heart
be troubled, neither let it be afraid."

John 14:27

FEAR

I sought You, LORD, and You heard me, and delivered me from all my fears.

Psalm 34:4

No weapon that is formed against me will prosper, and every tongue that will rise against me in judgment You will condemn. This is the heritage of Your servants, LORD, and my righteousness is of You.

Isaiah 54:17

"Fear not, for I am with you. Do not be dismayed, for I am your God. I will strengthen you; yes, I will help you; yes, I will uphold you with the right hand of My righteousness."

Isaiah 41:10

"Whoever hearkens to Me will dwell safely and will be quiet from fear of evil."

Proverbs 1:33

I have not received the spirit of bondage again to fear, but I have received the Spirit of adoption, by whom I cry, Abba, Father.

Romans 8:15

Fear

Though I walk through the valley of the shadow of
death, I will fear no evil, for You are with me. Your rod
and Your staff comfort me.

Psalm 23:4

The LORD is my light and my salvation; whom shall I
fear? The LORD is the strength of my life; of whom
shall I be afraid? Though an army should encamp
against me, my heart will not fear. Though war rises
against me, in this I will be confident.

Psalm 27:1,3

You are the LORD; You do not change.

Malachi 3:6

"For the oppression of the poor, for the sighing of the
needy, now will I arise," says the LORD; "I will set you
in safety from him that puffs at you."

Psalm 12:5

*The wise man in the storm prays to God, not for safety
from danger, but for deliverance from fear. It is the storm
within which endangers him, not the storm without..*

Ralph Waldo Emerson

FINANCES

I seek first Your kingdom, and Your righteousness; and all these things shall be added unto me.

Matthew 6:33

"Honor Me, Your LORD, with your substance and with the first of all your increase, so your barns will be filled with plenty and your presses will burst out with new wine."

Proverbs 3:9-10

You that spared not Your own Son, but delivered Him up for us all, how shall You not with Him also freely give me all things?

Romans 8:32

I know the grace of my Lord Jesus Christ, that, though He was rich, yet for my sake He became poor, that I through His poverty might be rich.

2 Corinthians 8:9

Riches and honor are with wisdom; yes, durable riches and righteousness. . . . Wisdom causes me who loves her to inherit substance; and she will fill my treasures.

Proverbs 8:18,21

FINANCES

Blessed am I who walks not in the counsel of the
ungodly, nor stands in the way of sinners or sits in the
seat of the scornful. But my delight is in Your law,
LORD, and in Your law I meditate day and night. . . .
And whatever I do will prosper.

Psalm 1:1-3

I give, and it shall be given unto me; good measure,
pressed down, and shaken together, and running over,
shall men give into my bosom. For with the same
measure that I measure out, it shall be measured to
me again.

Luke 6:38

One becomes poor who deals with a slack hand: but my
hand, the hand of the diligent, makes rich.

Proverbs 10:4

The house of the wicked shall be overthrown; but ours,
the tabernacle of the upright, shall flourish.

Proverbs 14:11

Finances

I will not be highminded, or trust in uncertain riches,
but in You, the living God, who gives me richly all
things to enjoy.

1 Timothy 6:17

I am poor and needy; yet You, LORD, think upon me:
You are my help and my deliverer; make no tarrying,
O my God.

Psalm 40:16

I take no thought for my life, what I shall eat: neither
for the body, what I shall put on. . . . But rather I seek
Your kingdom, God; and all these things shall be added
unto me. I fear not, for it is Your good pleasure, Father,
to give me the kingdom.

Luke 12:22,31-32

The one who has a bountiful eye shall be blessed
[including me]; for they give of their bread to the poor.

Proverbs 22:9

I trust in You, LORD, and do good; so shall I dwell in
the land, and I shall be fed.

Psalm 37:3

I say continually, "Be magnified, LORD, who has
pleasure in my prosperity as Your servant."

Psalm 35:27

In our house, the house of the righteous, is much
treasure: but in the revenues of the wicked is trouble.

Proverbs 15:6

In my prosperity . . . I shall never be moved.

Psalm 141:6

I bring all my tithes into the storehouse, that there may
be meat in Your house, and I prove You now with this,
LORD of hosts, that You will open to me the windows
of heaven, and pour me out a blessing, that there shall
not be room enough to receive it. And You will rebuke
the devourer for my sake.

Malachi 3:10

I have been young, and now am old; yet have I not seen
You forsake the righteous, nor have I seen their seed
begging bread.

Psalm 37:25

FINANCES

If I trust in my riches I shall fall: but I am righteous and shall flourish as a branch.

Proverbs 11:28

You wish above all things that I may prosper and be in health, even as my soul prospers.

3 John 2

Your blessing, LORD, makes me rich, and You add no sorrow with it.

Proverbs 10:22

The young lions do lack, and suffer hunger: but I seek You, LORD, and shall not want any good thing.

Psalm 34:10

Praise You, LORD. I am blessed because I fear You, LORD, because I delight greatly in Your commandments. . . . Wealth and riches shall be in my house: and my righteousness endures forever.

Psalm 112:1,3

You are my God, and You shall supply all my need according to Your riches in glory by Christ Jesus.

Philippians 4:19

Finances

If I sow sparingly I shall reap also sparingly; and if I sow bountifully I shall reap also bountifully. Every person according as they purpose in their heart so let them give, not grudgingly or of necessity, for You, God, love a cheerful giver. And You are able to make all grace abound toward me, so that I, always having all sufficiency in all things, may abound to every good work.

2 Corinthians 9:6-8

My eyes wait upon You; and You give me my meat in due season. You open Your hand, and satisfy the desire of every living thing.

Psalm 145:15-16

I am a strong person and retain riches.

Proverbs 11:14

I am upright so I shall have good things in possession.

Proverbs 28:10

*There is no portion of our time that is our time,
and the rest God's; there is no portion of money
that is our money, and the rest God's money. It is
all His; He made it all, gives it all, and He has
simply trusted it to us for His service. A servant has two
purses, the master's and his own, but we have only one.*

Adolphe Monod

GREED

"*H*aving food and clothes let yourself be content. But those who will be rich fall into temptation and a snare, and into many foolish and hurtful lusts, which drown people in destruction and ruin. For the love of money is the root of all evil, which while some coveted after, they have erred from the faith, and pierced themselves through with many sorrows. But you, O child of God, flee these things, and follow after righteousness."

1 Timothy 6:8-11

[The slothful] covets greedily all day long, but the righteous give and spare not.

Proverbs 21:26

Those who are greedy of gain trouble their own houses, but those who hate bribes shall live.

Proverbs 15:27

Hell and destruction are never full, so the eyes of people are never satisfied.

Proverbs 27:20

Greed

"Let your character be without covetousness and be content with such things as you have, for I have said, 'I will ever leave you, nor forsake you.'"

Hebrews 13:5

Godliness with contentment is great gain. For I brought nothing into this world, and it is certain I can carry nothing out.

1 Timothy 6:6-7

The cares of this world, and deceitfulness of riches, and the lusts of other things entering in, choke the word, and it becomes unfruitful. And these are they, which are sown on good ground, such as hear the word, and receive it, and bring forth fruit.

Mark 4:19-20

I do not speak in respect of want, for I have learned, in whatever state I am, to be content. I know how to be abased, and I know how to abound. . . . I can do all things through Christ who strengthens me.

Philippians 4:11-13

The covetous man pines in plenty, like
Tantalus up to the chin in water, and yet thirsty.
Thomas Adams

GRIEF

$\mathcal{H}$e is despised and rejected of men, a man of sorrow
and acquainted with grief. . . . Surely He has borne my
griefs and carried my sorrows.

                                            Isaiah 53:3-4

The Spirit of the Lord GOD is upon me; because the
LORD has anointed me to preach good tidings to the
meek; he has sent me to bind up the brokenhearted, to
proclaim liberty to the captives, and the opening of the
prison to those who are bound; to proclaim the
acceptable year of the LORD, and the day of vengeance
of our God; to comfort all who mourn; to appoint to
those who mourn in Zion, to give to them beauty for
ashes, the oil of joy for mourning, the garment of praise
for the spirit of heaviness; that they might be called
trees of righteousness, the planting of the LORD, that
He might be glorified.

                                            Isaiah 61:1-3

Grief

You heal the broken in heart and bind up their wounds.

Psalm 147:3

Your ransomed ones, LORD, shall return and come to Zion with songs and everlasting joy upon their heads. They shall obtain joy and gladness, and sorrow and sighing will flee away.

Isaiah 35:10

It is of Your mercies, LORD, that we are not consumed, because Your compassions do not fail. They are new every morning. Great is Your faithfulness.

Lamentations 3:22-23

My eye is consumed because of grief; it grows old because of all my enemies. Depart from me, all you workers of wrongdoing, for the LORD has heard the voice of my weeping. The LORD has heard my supplication; the LORD will receive my prayer.

Psalm 6:7-9

You will not break a bruised reed, and the smoking wick You will not quench. You will bring forth justice.

Isaiah 42:3

GRIEF

Blessed am I who mourn, for I will be comforted.

Matthew 5:4

Now our Lord Jesus Christ Himself and You, my
Father, have loved us and have given us everlasting
consolation and good hope through grace. Comfort our
hearts and establish us in every good word and work.

2 Thessalonians 2:16-17

I who sow in tears will reap in joy.

Psalm 126:5

"The redeemed of the LORD shall return and come
with singing to Zion, and everlasting joy will be upon
their heads. They shall obtain gladness and joy, and
sorrow and mourning shall flee away. I, even I, am He
who comforts you."

Isaiah 51:11-12

You, LORD, will comfort Zion. You will comfort all her
waste places, and You will make her wilderness like
Eden and her desert like Your garden, LORD. Joy and
gladness will be found there, thanksgiving and the voice
of melody.

Isaiah 51:3

GRIEF

You will swallow up death in victory, and You, Lord
GOD, will wipe away tears from off all faces . . . for
You, LORD, have spoken it.

Isaiah 25:8

LORD, You have comforted Your people and will have
mercy on Your afflicted. . . . "I have engraved you upon
the palms of My hands; your walls are continually
before Me."

Isaiah 49:13,16

Hear, O LORD, and have mercy on me. LORD, be my
helper. You have turned my mourning into dancing for
me. You have put off my sackcloth and surrounded me
with gladness.

Psalm 30:10-11

John saw the holy city, new Jerusalem, coming down
from You, God, out of heaven. . . . You, God, will wipe
away all tears from their eyes, and there will be no more
death, nor sorrow, nor crying, neither shall there be any
more pain, for the former things are passed away.

Revelation 21:2,4

Grief

I have called upon You, for You will hear me, O God.
Incline Your ear to me and hear my speech. . . . Keep
me as the apple of Your eye; hide me under the shadow
of Your wings. . . . As for me, I will behold Your face in
righteousness. I will be satisfied, when I awake, with
Your likeness.

Psalm 17:6,8,15

Blessed are You, God, even the Father of my Lord Jesus
Christ, Father of mercies and the God of all comfort.
You comfort me in all my tribulation, that I may be able
to comfort those who are in any trouble by the comfort
with which I myself am comforted by You.

2 Corinthians 1:3-4

It is in dying that we are born to eternal life.

St. Francis of Assisi

ILLNESS

$\mathcal{T}$he one who dwells in Your secret place, most High, will abide under Your shadow, Almighty. . . . There will no evil befall them, neither will any plague come near their dwelling.

Psalm 91:1,10

LORD, You open the eyes of the blind. You raise them up who are bowed down. You love the righteous [including me].

Psalm 146:8

Fools [even me] are afflicted. . . . You sent Your word and healed me and delivered me from my destruction.

Psalm 107:17,20

Heal me, O LORD, and I shall be healed. Save me, and I shall be saved, for You are my praise.

Jeremiah 17:14

Is any sick among you? Let him call for the elders of the church, and let them pray over them, anointing them with oil in the name of the Lord. And the prayer of faith will save the sick, and the Lord shall raise them up.

James 5:14-15

ILLNESS

"My child, attend to my words; incline your ear to my
sayings. Do not let them depart from your eyes. Keep
them in the midst of your heart. For they are life to
those who find them and health to all their flesh."

Proverbs 4:20-22

Himself bore our sins in His own body on the tree so
that we, being dead to sins, should live to righteousness.
By His stripes we were healed.

1 Peter 2:24

"Because you have set your love upon Me, therefore will
I deliver you. I will set you on high, because you have
known My name. . . . With long life will I satisfy you
and show you My salvation."

Psalm 91:14,16

Though I walk through the valley of the shadow of
death, I will fear no evil, for You are with me. Your rod
and Your staff comfort me.

Psalm 23:4

ILLNESS

Bless the LORD, O my soul, and do not forget all His
benefits, who forgives all my offenses, who heals all
my diseases.

Psalm 103:2-3

Why are you downcast, O my soul? And why are you
disquieted within me? Hope in God, for I will yet
praise Him, who is the health of my countenance and
my God.

Psalm 43:5

"If you will diligently hearken to the voice of the LORD
your God and will do that which is right in My sight
and will give ear to My commandments and keep all
My statutes, I will put none of these diseases upon you,
which I have brought upon the Egyptians, for I am the
LORD who heals you."

Exodus 15:26

"I was wounded for your transgressions, I was bruised
for your offenses. The punishment for your peace was
upon Me, and with My stripes you are healed."

Isaiah 53:5

ILLNESS

LORD, You preserve the simple. I was brought low and You helped me. . . . I will walk before You, LORD, in the land of the living.

> Psalm 116:6,9

A merry heart [even mine] does good like a medicine, but a broken spirit dries the bones.

> Proverbs 17:22

"To you who fear My name will the Sun of righteousness arise with healing in His wings; and you will go forth and grow up as calves of the stall."

> Malachi 4:2

I am blessed who consider the poor. You, LORD, will deliver me in time of trouble. You will preserve me and keep me alive, and I shall be blessed upon the earth, and You will not deliver me into the will of my enemies. LORD, You will strengthen me upon the bed of languishing. You will restore me on my bed of sickness.

> Psalm 41:1-3

A sound heart is the life of the flesh, but envy, the rottenness of the bones.

> Proverbs 14:30

ILLNESS

"You shall serve Me, the LORD your God, and I shall
bless your bread and your water, and I will take sickness
away from your midst."

Exodus 23:25-26

God, You anointed Jesus of Nazareth with the Holy
Spirit and with power, who went about doing good and
healing all who were oppressed of the devil, for You
were with Him.

Acts 10:38

"O Israel, you have destroyed yourself, but in Me is your
help. . . . I will ransom you from the power of the grave;
I will redeem you from death. O death, I will be your
plagues; O grave, I will be your destruction."

Hosea 13:9,14

He is a path, if any be misled;
He is a robe, if any naked be;
If any chance to hunger, He is bread;
If any be a bondman, He is free;
If any be but weak, how strong is He!
To dead men, life is He; to sick men, health;
To blind men, sight; and to the needy, wealth;
A pleasure without loss; a treasure without stealth.

Giles Fletcher

Impure Thoughts

As one thinks in their heart, so are they.

Proverbs 23:7

Though we walk in the flesh, we do not war after the flesh. (For the weapons of our warfare are not carnal, but mighty through You, God, to the pulling down of strongholds;) casting down imaginations, and every high thing that exalts itself against the knowledge of You, God, and bringing into captivity every thought to the obedience of Christ.

2 Corinthians 10:3-5

"Present your bodies a living sacrifice, holy, acceptable to Me, which is your reasonable service. And do not be conformed to this world, but be transformed by the renewing of your mind, that you may prove what is that good, and acceptable, and perfect, will of God."

Romans 12:1-3

IMPURE THOUGHTS

Wash me thoroughly from my offense, and cleanse me from my sin. For I acknowledge my transgressions, and my sin is ever before me. Against You, You only, have I sinned.

Psalm 51:2-4

"Whatever things are . . . pure . . . lovely . . . if there be any virtue, and if there be any praise, think on these things. Those things, which you have both learned, and received, and heard, and seen in me, do; and I, the God of peace shall be with you."

Philippians 4:8-9

Your law, LORD, is perfect, converting my soul. . . . The fear of You, LORD, is clean, enduring forever.

Psalm 19:7,9

How shall a young person cleanse their way? By taking heed to it according to Your word. . . . Your word, LORD, have I hid in my heart, that I might not sin against You.

Psalm 119:9,11

IMPURE THOUGHTS

If I confess my sins, You are faithful and just to forgive me my sin, and to cleanse me from all unrighteousness.

1 John 1:9

I hate vain thoughts, but Your law do I love. You are my hiding place and my shield. I hope in Your word. . . . Uphold me according to Your word, that I may live. . . . Hold me up, and I shall be safe.

Psalm 119:113-114,116-117

Cleanse me from secret faults. Keep me, Your servant, back also from presumptuous sins. Do not let them have dominion over me. Then I shall be upright. . . . Let the words of my mouth, and the meditation of my heart, be acceptable in Your sight, O LORD, my strength, and my redeemer.

Psalm 19:12-14

A person's mind is the Holy of Holies,
and to admit evil thoughts
is like setting up an idol in the temple..
The Berdichever Rabbi

INJUSTICE

*W*hen I cry to You, then will my enemies turn back.
This I know; for, God, You are for me.

Psalm 56:9

I who love Your law have great peace, and nothing will
offend me.

Psalm 119:165

It is thankworthy if I for conscience toward You endure
grief, suffering wrongfully. For what glory is it, if, when
I am beaten for my faults, I shall take it patiently? But
if, when I do well, I suffer for it, I take it patiently, this
is acceptable with You, God.

1 Peter 2:19-20

"If the world hates you, you know that it hated Me
before it hated you. If you were of the world, the world
would love its own; but because you are not of the
world, the world hates you."

John 15:18-19

You, LORD, execute righteousness and judgment for all
who are oppressed [even me].

Psalm 103:6

Injustice

Evildoers will be cut off, but I who wait upon You,
LORD, shall inherit the earth.

Psalm 37:9

LORD, You prepare a table before me in the presence of
my enemies. You anoint my head with oil; my cup runs
over. Surely goodness and mercy will follow me all the
days of my life, and I will dwell in the house of the
LORD forever.

Psalm 23:5-6

"Do not render evil for evil or insult for insult, but on
the contrary, blessing, knowing that you are called to
this, that you should inherit a blessing. For the one who
will love life and see good days, let them refrain their
tongue from evil and their lips from speaking guile. Let
them shun evil and do good; let them seek peace and
pursue it."

1 Peter 3:9-11

God, You will bring every work into judgment, with
every secret thing, whether it is good or whether it
is evil.

Ecclesiastes 12:14

173

INJUSTICE

I am blessed when men will defame, persecute, and say
all kinds of evil things against me falsely, for Jesus'
sake. I rejoice and am very glad for great is my reward
in heaven, for in the same way they persecuted the
prophets who were before me.

Matthew 5:11-12

Those who hate me without a cause are more than the
hairs of my head. Those who would destroy me, being
my enemies wrongfully, are mighty. . . . LORD, You hear
the poor and do not despise Your prisoners. . . . God,
You will save Zion and will build the cities of Judah,
that they may dwell there and possess it.

Psalm 69:4,33,35

Who will lay anything to the charge of Your elect, God?
It is You who justify. Who is the one who condemns?
It is Christ who died, yes rather, that is risen again,
who is even at the right hand of God, who also makes
intercession for us.

Romans 8:33-34

INJUSTICE

"'I will deliver you in that day,' says the LORD. 'And you shall not be given into the hand of the people of whom you are afraid. For I will surely deliver you, and you will not fall by the sword . . . because you have put your trust in Me,' says the LORD."

Jeremiah 39:17-18

"All who are incensed against you will be ashamed and put to confusion. They will be as nothing, and those who strive with you will perish. You will seek them and will not find them, even those who contended with you. Those who war against you will be as nothing and as a nonexistent thing. For I, the Lord your God, will hold your right hand, saying to you, 'Do not fear; I will help you.'"

Isaiah 41:11-13

I will not be afraid of ten thousands of people, who have set themselves against me all around. Arise, O Lord; save me, O my God. For You have smitten all my enemies upon the cheekbone; You have broken the teeth of the ungodly. Salvation belongs to You, Lord. Your blessing is upon your people.

Psalm 3:6-8

INJUSTICE

[Jesus said,] "Will not God avenge His own elect, who cry day and night to Him, though He bears a long time with them? I tell you that He will avenge them speedily."

Luke 18:7-8

In the time of trouble, You will hide me in Your pavilion. In the secret of Your tabernacle will You hide me. You will set me up upon a rock. Now my head will be lifted up above my enemies all around me; therefore, I will offer in Your tabernacle sacrifices of joy. I will sing, yes, I will sing praise to You, LORD.

Psalm 27:5-6

Flee a thousand leagues from saying, "I was in the right. It was not right for me to suffer this. They had no right to treat me so." God deliver us from all such rights. And when we receive honors, or affection, or kind treatment, let us ask what right we have to them.

Saint Teresa of Avila

JEALOUSY

LORD, the fear of You leads to life, and the one
who has it will abide satisfied. They will not be visited
with evil.

Proverbs 19:23

Godliness with contentment is great gain. For I brought
nothing into this world, and it is certain I can carry
nothing out.

1 Timothy 6:6-7

"I will satisfy the soul of the priests with abundance,
and My people shall be satisfied with My goodness,'
says the LORD."

Jeremiah 31:14

"Let your character be without covetousness; and be
content with the things you have, for I have said, 'I will
never leave you nor forsake you.'"

Hebrews 13:5

"Do not let your heart envy sinners, but be in the fear
of Me, Your LORD, all day long. For surely there is a
future, and your expectation will not be cut off."

Proverbs 23:17-18

JEALOUSY

You satisfy my mouth with good things so that my
youth is renewed like the eagle's.

Psalm 103:5

Better is a handful with quietness, than both hands full
with travail and annoyance.

Ecclesiastes 4:6

Because Your lovingkindness is better than life, my lips
shall praise You. Thus I will bless You while I live. I will
lift up my hands in Your name. My soul will be satisfied
as with the best foods; and my mouth will praise You
with joyful lips.

Psalm 63:3-5

"Rest in the Me, your LORD, and wait patiently for
Me. Do not fret because of the one who prospers in
their way, because of the one who brings wicked devices
to pass. . . . For evildoers will be cut off, but those who
wait on Me shall inherit the earth."

Psalm 37:7,9

JEALOUSY

I who am Christ's have crucified the flesh with the affections and lusts. If I live in the Spirit, let me also walk in the Spirit. Let me not be conceited, provoking others, envying others.

Galatians 5:24-26

Do not envy the oppressor, and do not choose any of his ways. For the perverse is an abomination to the LORD, but His secret is with the righteous [even me].

Proverbs 3:31-32

"If you have bitter envy and strife in your hearts, do not glory in it and do not lie against the truth. This wisdom does not descend from above, but is earthly, sensual, devilish."

James 3:14-15

Love does not envy.

1 Corinthians 13:4

A sound heart is the life of my flesh, but envy, rottenness to my bones.

Proverbs 14:30

The jealous are troublesome to others,
a torment to themselves.

William Penn

LONELINESS

*K*now that the LORD is God. It is He who has made us and not we ourselves; we are Your people and the sheep of Your pasture.

Psalm 100:3

"Look, I stand at the door and knock. If anyone hears My voice and opens the door, I will come into him and will eat with him and he with Me."

Revelation 3:20

"You are My friends if you do whatever I command you. From now on I do not call you servants, for the servant does not know what his lord does, but I have called you friends, for all things that I have heard of My Father I have made known to you. You have not chosen Me, but I have chosen you."

John 15:14-16

"I am with you always, even until the end of the world."

Matthew 28:20

LONELINESS

A father of the fatherless and a judge of the widows are You in Your holy habitation, God. You set the solitary in families. You bring out those who are bound with chains, but the rebellious dwell in a dry land.

Psalm 68:5-6

Two are better than one, because they have a good reward for their labor. For if they fall, the one will lift up their fellow. But woe to the one who is alone when they fall, for they do not have another to help them up. Again, if two lie together, then they have heat, but how can one be warm alone? And if one prevail against one, two shall withstand the one; and a threefold cord is not quickly broken.

Ecclesiastes 4:9-12

"I will not leave you comfortless. I will come to you."

John 14:18

LONELINESS

LORD, You are good to those who wait for You, to the soul who seeks You.

Lamentations 3:25

LORD, You preserve the strangers; You relieve the fatherless and widow; but the way of the wicked You turn upside down.

Psalm 146:9

"Can a woman forget her sucking child, that she should not have compassion on the son of her womb? Yes, they may forget, yet I will not forget you. Look, I have engraved you on the palms of My hands; your walls are continually before Me."

Isaiah 49:15-16

My God, You shall supply all my need according to Your riches in glory by Christ Jesus.

Philippians 4:19

You, LORD, are near to all who call on You, to all who call upon You in truth.

Psalm 145:18

One who has friends must show himself friendly, and there is a friend who sticks closer than a brother.

Proverbs 18:24

LONELINESS

"I will betroth you to Myself forever; yes, I will betroth
you in righteousness, and in judgment, and in loving
kindness, and in mercies. I will even betroth you to
Myself in faithfulness, and you will know the LORD."

Hosea 2:19-20

He has said, "I will never leave you, nor forsake you."

Hebrews 13:5

"Draw near to Me, your God, and I will draw near
to you."

James 4:8

What person is the one who fears You, LORD? This
one shall You teach in the way that they shall choose.
Their soul will dwell at ease, and their seed will inherit
the earth.

Psalm 25:12-13

"'Come out from among them, and be separate,' says the
Lord; 'and do not touch the unclean thing, and I will
receive you, and will be a Father to you, and you will be
My sons and daughters,' says the Lord Almighty."

2 Corinthians 6:17-18

Loneliness

"You will call and I, your LORD, will answer; you will
cry, and I will say, 'Here I am.'"

Isaiah 58:9

I am complete in [Christ], who is the head of all
principality and power.

Colossians 2:10

"Where two or three are gathered together in My name,
I am there in the midst of them."

Matthew 18:20

My soul longs, yes, even faints for Your courts, LORD.
My heart and my flesh cry out for You, the living God.
. . . They are blessed who dwell in Your house. They
will be ever praising You. . . . For a day in Your courts
is better than a thousand. I had rather be a doorkeeper
in Your house, God, than to dwell in the tents
of wickedness.

Psalm 84:2,4,10

*In every man there is a loneliness, an inner chamber
of peculiar life into which God only can enter.*
George Macdonald

LOSS

I would not have you to be ignorant, fellow believers, concerning those who are asleep, that you not have sorrow, even as others who have no hope. For if we believe that Jesus died and rose again, even so those also who sleep in Jesus will God bring with Him.

1 Thessalonians 4:13-14

The righteous perish and no one lays it to heart, and merciful people are taken away, none considering that the righteous is taken away from the evil to come. They shall enter into peace; they shall rest in their beds, each one walking in uprightness.

Isaiah 57:1-2

"The thief comes only to steal, kill, and destroy. I am come that you might have life and that you might have it more abundantly."

John 10:10

In the day of trouble I call upon You, for You will answer me.

Psalm 86:7

LOSS

"I will restore to you the years that the locust has
eaten . . . and you shall eat plenty and be satisfied
and praise the name of the LORD your God who has
dealt wondrously with you; and My people shall never
be ashamed."

Joel 2:25-26

I am poor and sorrowful; let Your salvation, O God, set
me up on high. I will praise Your name, God, with a
song and will magnify You with thanksgiving. . . . The
humble will see this and be glad. And my heart will
live who seeks You, for You hear the poor.

Psalm 69:29-30,32-33

The sorrows of death surround me. . . . In my distress,
I called upon You, LORD, and cried to You, my God.
You heard my voice out of Your temple, and my cry
came before You, into Your ears.

Psalm 18:4,6

Loss

O death, where is your sting? O grave, where is your victory? The sting of death is sin, and the strength of sin is the law. But thanks be, God, to You who gives me the victory through my Lord Jesus Christ.

1 Corinthians 15:55-57

"There is no one who has left house, or brothers, or sisters, or father, or mother, or wife, or children, or lands, for My sake, and the gospel's, but that person shall receive a hundredfold now in this time, houses, and brothers, and sisters, and mothers, and children, and lands, with persecutions; and in the world to come eternal life."

Mark 10:29-30

The wicked is driven away in his wickedness; but the righteous has hope [even] in death.

Proverbs 14:32

God has a bottle and a book for his people's tears.
What was sown as a tear will come up as a pearl.
Matthew Henry

MISTAKES

$\mathcal{W}$ho is the one who condemns? It is Christ who
died, yes, rather who is risen again, who is even at Your
right hand making intercession for me.

> Romans 8:34

"Return to me, the LORD your God. . . . I will heal
your backsliding, I will love you freely, for My anger is
turned away from you."

> Hosea 14:1,4

Don't rejoice against me, O my enemy, for when I fall,
I shall arise; when I sit in darkness, the LORD shall be
a light to me.

> Micah 7:8

LORD, You uphold all who fall and raise up all who are
bowed down [even me].

> Psalm 145:14

Thanks be to You, God, who always causes me to
triumph in Christ.

> 2 Corinthians 2:14

A just person falls seven times, and rises up again.

> Proverbs 24:16

MISTAKES

"When you pass through the waters, I will be with you; and through the rivers, they will not overflow you. When you walk through the fire, you shall not be burned nor will the flame consume you. For I am the LORD your God, the Holy One of Israel, your Savior."

Isaiah 43:2-3

Lord, You are good and ready to forgive. You are abundant in mercy to all who call on You.

Psalm 86:5

LORD, You are gracious and full of compassion; slow to get angry and of great mercy.

Psalm 145:8

The one who covers his sins will not prosper, but whoever confesses and forsakes them will have mercy.

Proverbs 28:13

Who is a God like You, who pardons offense and passes by the transgression of the remnant of His heritage? You do not retain your anger forever because You delight in mercy.

Micah 7:18-19

MISTAKES

"Return, you backsliding child, and I will heal your
backslidings." Behold, I come to you; for you are the
LORD my God.

Jeremiah 3:22

All have sinned and come short of Your glory, God.
You have justified me freely by Your grace through
the redemption that is in Christ Jesus.

Romans 3:23-24

"Humble yourself under the mighty hand of your God
so that I may exalt you in due time."

1 Peter 5:6

Like a father has compassion on his children, so You,
LORD, have compassion on me, who fears You. For
You know my frame; You remember that I am dust.

Psalm 103:13-14

If I confess my sins, You are faithful and just to forgive
me my sins and to cleanse me from all unrighteousness.

1 John 1:9

Bless the LORD, O my soul. . . . [He] redeems my life
from destruction; [He] crowns me with lovingkindness
and tender mercies.

Psalm 103:1,4

MISTAKES

All things work together for good to those who love
You and who are called according to Your purpose.

Romans 8:28

You will have compassion on me according to the
multitude of Your mercies.

Lamentations 3:32

You have made me a little lower than the angels and
have crowned me with glory and honor. You made me
to have dominion over the works of Your hands. You
have put all things under my feet.

Psalm 8:5-6

You, LORD, will bless the righteous; with favor you will
surround me as with a shield.

Psalm 5:12

LORD, how are they increased who trouble me! Many
are they who rise up against me. Many are there who
say of my soul, "There is no help for this one in God."
But You, O LORD, are a shield for me, my glory and
the lifter up of my head. I cried to You, LORD, with my
voice, and You heard me out of Your holy hill.

Psalm 3:1-4

MISTAKES

I am confident of this very thing, that You who have begun a good work in me will perform it until the day of Jesus Christ.

Philippians 1:6

Who shall separate me from the love of Christ? Shall tribulation, or distress, or persecution, or famine, or nakedness, or peril, or sword? . . . No, in all these things, I am more than a conqueror through Him who loved me.

Romans 8:35,37

Though I fall, I shall not be utterly cast down, for You, LORD, uphold me with Your hand.

Psalm 37:24

LORD, You take pleasure in those who fear You and in those who hope in Your mercy.

Psalm 147:11

To make no mistakes is not in the power of man;
but from their errors and mistakes
the wise and good learn wisdom for the future.

Plutarch

PRIDE

"*H*umble yourselves in the sight of your Lord, and I will lift you up."

James 4:10

Pride goes before destruction, and a haughty spirit before a fall. It is better [for me] to be of a humble spirit with the lowly, than to divide the spoil with the proud.

Proverbs 16:18-19

Father, all that is in the world, the lust of the flesh, and the lust of the eyes, and the pride of life, is not of You but is of the world. And the world passes away and the lust of it, but God, the one who does Your will abides forever.

1 John 2:16-17

Before destruction the heart of a person is haughty, and before honor is humility.

Proverbs 18:12

You will save the afflicted people but will bring down high looks.

Psalm 18:27

Pride

In the mouth of the foolish is a rod of pride, but the lips of the wise will preserve them.

Proverbs 14:3

When pride comes, then comes shame, but with the lowly is wisdom.

Proverbs 11:2

[Hannah prayed and said,] "Talk no more so exceeding proudly; do not let arrogance come out of your mouth, for the LORD is a God of knowledge, and by Him actions are weighed."

1 Samuel 2:3

With the merciful You will show Yourself merciful, and with the upright one You will show Yourself upright. With the pure You will show Yourself pure, and with the perverse You will show Yourself shrewd. And the afflicted people You will save, but Your eyes are upon the haughty, that You may bring them down.

2 Samuel 22:26-28

He that is down needs fear no fall,
He that is low, no pride;
He that is humble ever shall
Have God to be his guide.

John Bunyan

REJECTION

My own familiar friend, in whom I trusted, who ate of my bread, has lifted up his heel against me. But You, O LORD, be merciful to me and raise me up, that I may repay them. By this I know that You favor me: because my enemy does not triumph over me.

Psalm 41:9-11

"You are blessed who are persecuted for righteousness' sake, for the kingdom of heaven is yours."

Matthew 5:10

I will also be a crown of glory in the hand of the LORD, and a royal diadem in the hand of God. I shall no longer be called Forsaken; neither shall my land anymore be termed Desolate . . . for the LORD delights in me.

Isaiah 62:3-4

You are a gracious and merciful God . . . who keeps covenant and mercy.

Nehemiah 9:31-32

REJECTION

I will call on You, LORD; who are worthy to be praised.
So I will be saved from my enemies.

Psalm 18:3

Do not let mercy and truth forsake you. Bind them
around your neck; write them on the table of your heart,
so you will find favor and good understanding in the
sight of God and man.

Proverbs 3:3-4

"If from now on you shall seek the LORD your God,
you will find Me, if you seek Me with all your heart and
with all your soul. When you are in tribulation and all
these things have come upon you, even in the latter
days, if you turn to the LORD your God and will be
obedient to My voice, (for I, the LORD your God, am a
merciful God); I will not forsake you, neither destroy
you, nor forget the covenant of your fathers which I
swore to them."

Deuteronomy 4:29-31

REJECTION

"'I will restore health to you and I will heal you of your wounds,' says the LORD, 'because they called you an outcast.'"

Jeremiah 30:17

I have received the Spirit of adoption, by whom I cry, "Abba, Father." The Spirit Himself bears witness with my spirit that I am Your child, God.

Romans 8:15-16

He is despised and rejected of men, a man of sorrows and acquainted with grief . . . He was despised. . . . Surely He has borne my griefs and carried my sorrows. . . . He was wounded for my transgressions, He was bruised for my offenses. The punishment for my peace was upon Him, and with His stripes I am healed.

Isaiah 53:3-5

"All who the Father gives Me will come to Me, and those who come to Me I will in no way cast out."

John 6:37

REJECTION

Let all who put their trust in You rejoice. Let them ever shout for joy, because You defend them. Let those also who love Your name be joyful in You. For You, LORD, will bless the righteous; You surround them with favor as with a shield.

Psalm 5:11-12

LORD, when our ways please You, You make even our enemies to be at peace with us.

Proverbs 16:7

LORD, You will not cast off Your people [including me], neither will You forsake Your inheritance.

Psalm 94:14

Fools make a mock at sin, but among the righteous there is favor.

Proverbs 14:9

LORD, You will not forsake Your people for Your great name's sake, because it has pleased You to make us Your people.

1 Samuel 12:22

No one understands you, your friends reproach;
but your Maker draws nigh, and gives you a song—
a song of hope, the song which is harmonious
with the strong, deep music of His providence.
Be ready to sing the songs that your Maker gives.

Lettie B. Cowman

RELATIONSHIPS

"*I*f two of you shall agree on earth as touching anything that they shall ask, it shall be done for them by my Father who is in heaven. For where two or three are gathered together in My name, there I am in the midst of them."

Matthew 18:19-20

"Servants, [or employees,] obey in all things your masters [bosses] according to the flesh, not with eyeservice as a man-pleaser, but in singleness of heart, fearing Me, your God. And whatever you do, do it heartily as to your Lord and not to people, knowing that from Me, your Lord, you will receive the reward of the inheritance, for you serve the Lord Christ."

Colossians 3:22-24

God, You are faithful, by whom I am called to the fellowship of Your Son, Jesus Christ my Lord.

1 Corinthians 1:9

RELATIONSHIPS

Two are better than one, because they have a good
reward for their labor. For if they fall, the one will lift
up his companion, but woe to the one who is alone
when they fall, for they do not have another to help
them up. Again, if two lie together, then they have heat;
but how can one be warm alone? And if one prevail
against one, two shall withstand them, and a threefold
cord is not quickly broken.

Ecclesiastes 4: 9-12

"Honor your father and mother, which is the first
commandment with the promise, that it may be well
with you, and you may live long on the earth."

Ephesians 6:2-3

Through wisdom is my house built; and by
understanding it is established; and by knowledge
shall the chambers be filled with all precious and
pleasant riches.

Proverbs 24:3-4

If I walk in the light as He is in the light, I have
fellowship with others.

1 John 1:7

Relationships

[Paul wrote:] "Do not be unequally yoked together with unbelievers, for what fellowship has righteousness with unrighteousness? And what communion has light with darkness? . . . As God has said, 'I will dwell in them and walk in them; and I will be their God, and they will be my people.' 'Come out from among them and be separate,' says the Lord, 'and do not touch the unclean thing; and I will receive you, and will be a Father to you, and you will be my sons and daughters.'"

2 Corinthians 6:14-18

A good person leaves an inheritance to his children's children.

Proverbs 13:22

Children's children are the crown of old age; and the glory of children are their parents.

Proverbs 17:6

"Do not forsake your own friend and your father's friend; nor go into your brother's house in the day of calamity, for better is a neighbor who is near than a brother far off."

Proverbs 27:10

RELATIONSHIPS

"The LORD says to the eunuchs who keep My
Sabbaths, and choose the things that please Me, and
take hold of My covenant. Even to them will I give in
My house and within My walls a place and a name
better than of sons and of daughters. I will give them
an everlasting name, that will not be cut off."

Isaiah 56:4-5

"The sons of the stranger, that join themselves to the
LORD, to serve Him, and to love the name of the
LORD, to be His servants, everyone who keeps the
Sabbath from polluting it, and takes hold of My
covenant; even those will I bring to My holy mountain,
and make them joyful in My house of prayer. Their
burnt offerings and their sacrifices will be accepted on
My altar, for My house shall be called a house of prayer
for all people."

Isaiah 56:6-7

RELATIONSHIPS

Then will the King say to them on His right hand,
"Come, you blessed of My Father, inherit the kingdom
prepared for you from the foundation of the world,
for I was hungry, and you gave me meat; I was thirsty,
and you gave me drink; I was a stranger, and you took
me in."

Matthew 25:34-36

Jesus said to him, "You shall love the Lord your God
with all your heart, and with all your soul, and with all
your mind. This is the first and great commandment.
The second is like it, You shall love your neighbor as
yourself. On these two commandments hang all the
law and the prophets."

Matthew 22:37-40

Let us be first to give a friendship sign,
to nod first, smile first, speak first, and if
such a thing is necessary—forgive first.

Unknown

SELF-ESTEEM

*S*how Your marvelous lovingkindness, O You who
save by Your right hand those who put their trust in
You from those who rise up against them. Keep me
as the apple of the eye, hide me under the shadow of
Your wings.

Psalm 17:7-8

"Thus says the LORD who created you, O Jacob, and
He who formed You, O Israel, 'Fear not, for I have
redeemed you. I have called you by your name; You
are Mine.'"

Isaiah 43:1

How precious also are Your thoughts to me, O God!
How great is the sum of them! If I should count them,
they are more in number than the sand. When I awake,
I am still with You.

Psalm 139:17

"Behold, I have engraved you upon the palms of My
hands. Your walls are continually before me."

Isaiah 49:16

Self-esteem

What is man, that You are mindful of him? And the son of man, that You visit him? For You have made him a little lower than the angels, and have crowned him with glory and honor. You made him to have dominion over the works of your hands. You have put all things under his feet.

Psalm 8:4-6

The LORD has appeared of old to me, saying, "Yea, I have loved you with an everlasting love. Therefore with lovingkindness have I drawn you."

Jeremiah 31:3

I will praise You, for I am fearfully and wonderfully made. Marvelous are Your works, and that my soul knows right well.

Psalm 139:13

Consider then thyself, O noble soul, and the nobility within thee, for thou art honored above all creatures in that thou art an image of God; . . . thou art destined to greatness!
Meister Eckhart

SELFISHNESS

"*G*ive and it will be given to you—good measure,
pressed down, shaken together, and running over,
will be given to you. For with the same measure that
you measure, it shall be measured to you as well."

Luke 6:38

"Whoever will be great among you, shall be your
minister, and whoever of you will be the first, shall be
servant of all. For even the Son of man did not come to
be ministered to, but to minister, and to give His life a
ransom for many."

Mark 10:43-45

"All things whatever you would that others should
do to you, do even so to them, for this is the law and
the prophets."

Matthew 7:12

"To whomever much is given, much shall be required."

Luke 12:48

SELFISHNESS

Whoever has pity on the poor lends to You, LORD, and that which one has given will You pay [the giver] again.

Proverbs 19:17

The righteous [including me] consider the cause of the poor, but the wicked do not regard to know it.

Proverbs 29:7

"Since you have done it to one of the least of these My brothers, you have done it to Me."

Matthew 25:40

The one who gives to the poor shall not lack, but the one who hides his eyes shall have many curses.

Proverbs 28:27

The one who stops his ears at the cry of the poor shall also cry himself, but shall not be heard.

Proverbs 21:13

The one who has a bountiful eye shall be blessed, for he gives of his bread to the poor.

Proverbs 22:9

SELFISHNESS

"Let nothing be done through strife or vainglory, but in
lowliness of mind, let each esteem others better than
themselves. . . . Do not look on your own things, but
also on the things of others. Let this mind be in you,
which was also in Christ Jesus, who, being in the form
of God . . . made Himself of no reputation, and took
upon Himself the form of a servant."

Philippians 2:3-7

[Paul said:] "I have shown you all things, how that so
laboring you ought to support the weak, and to
remember the words of the Lord Jesus, how He said,
'It is more blessed to give than to receive.'"

Acts 20:35

Love . . . does not seek its own way.

1 Corinthians 13:4-5

*What we have done for ourselves alone dies
with us; what we have done for others
and the world remains and is eternal.*

Albert Pike

SHAME

$\mathcal{T}$hey looked to You and were lightened, and their faces were not ashamed. This poor person cried, and LORD, You heard me and saved me out of all my troubles.

Psalm 34:5-6

If we walk in the light as He is in the light, we have fellowship one with another and the blood of Jesus Christ His Son cleanses us from all sin.

1 John 1:7

I am poor and needy, yet Lord, You think about me. You are my help and my deliverer; do not delay, O my God.

Psalm 40:17

With the pure, You will show Yourself pure; and with the distorted, You will show Yourself shrewd. For You will save the afflicted people, but will bring down high looks. For You will light my candle. You, the LORD my God, will enlighten my darkness.

Psalm 18:26-28

Shame

I am the temple of the living God, as You have said, "I will dwell in them and walk in them; and I will be their God, and they will be my people." . . . Having Your promises, I cleanse myself from all filthiness of the flesh and spirit, perfecting holiness in the fear of You, God.

2 Corinthians 6:16, 7:1

[As the bride of the Lamb,] to me was granted to be arrayed in fine linen, clean and white, for fine linen is the righteousness of saints.

Revelation 19:8

Christ loved the church [which includes me] and gave Himself for it, that He might sanctify and cleanse it with the washing of water by the word, that He might present it to Himself a glorious church, not having spot or wrinkle or any such thing, but that it should be holy and without blemish.

Ephesians 5:25-27

SHAME

"I will sprinkle clean water upon you, and you will be clean; from all your filthiness and from all your idols, I will cleanse you. A new heart also will I give you, and a new spirit will I put within you; and I will take away the stony heart out of your flesh, and I will give you a heart of flesh. And I will put My Spirit within you and cause you to walk in My statutes, and you will keep my judgments and do them. . . . I will also save you from all your uncleanness."

Ezekiel 36:25-27,29

"I will cleanse you from all your wrongdoing, by which you have sinned against Me; and I will pardon all your offenses, by which you have sinned and by which you have transgressed against Me."

Jeremiah 33:8

SHAME

[Jesus said,] "Now you are clean through the word which I have spoken to you."

John 15:3

Truly You are good to Israel, even to such as are of a clean heart [even me].

Psalm 73:1

The fear of You, LORD, is clean, enduring forever; Your judgments are true and righteous altogether.

Psalm 19:9

The king's favor is toward a wise servant, but his wrath is against him who causes shame.

Proverbs 14:35

Purge me with hyssop, and I will be clean. Wash me, and I will be whiter than snow.

Psalm 51:7

"They shall not defile themselves anymore with their idols, nor with their detestable things, nor with any of their transgressions. But I will save them out of all their dwelling places, in which they have sinned, and will cleanse them, so they will be My people. And I will be their God."

Ezekiel 37:23

SHAME

"The LORD your God in the midst of you is mighty;
He will save, He will rejoice over you with joy; He will
rest in His love, He will joy over you with singing. I will
gather them who are sorrowful for the solemn assembly,
who are of you to whom the reproach of it was a
burden. Look, at that time I will undo all who afflict
you, and I will save the one who halts and gather the
one who was driven out; and I will get them praise and
fame in every land where they have been put to shame."

Zephaniah 3:17-19

[LORD,] draw near to my soul and redeem it. Deliver
me because of my enemies. You have known my
reproach, and my shame, and my dishonor. My
adversaries are all before You.

Psalm 69:18-19

A gracious woman retains honor, and strong men
retain riches.

Proverbs 11:16

Sanctify yourselves therefore, and be holy, for I am the
LORD your God. And you shall keep My statutes and
do them. I am the LORD who sanctifies you.

Leviticus 20:7-8

SHAME

The Scripture says, "Whoever believes on Him will not
be ashamed."

Romans 10:11

Then I will not be ashamed, when I have respect for
all Your commandments. . . . How shall a young person
cleanse his way? By taking heed to it according to
Your word.

Psalm 119:6,9

It is written, "Look, I lay in Zion a stumblingstone and
a rock of offence, and whoever believes on Him shall
not be ashamed."

Romans 9:33

*True humility accepts the love that is bestowed upon it, and
the gifts of that love, with a meek and happy thankfulness,
while pride shrinks from accepting gifts and kindnesses,
and is afraid to believe in the disinterested goodness of
the one who bestows them. Were we truly humble, we
would accept God's love with thankful meekness, and,
while acknowledging our own unworthiness, would
only think of it as enhancing His grace and goodness
in choosing us as the recipients of such blessings.*

Hannah Whitall Smith

STRESS

We would not, fellow believers, have you ignorant of our trouble which came to us in Asia, that we were pressed out of measure, above strength, so much so that we despaired even of life. But we had the sentence of death in ourselves, that we should not trust in ourselves, but in God who raises the dead, who delivered us from so great a death and does deliver, in whom we trust that He will yet deliver us.

2 Corinthians 1:8-10

"Come to me, all you who labor and are heavy laden, and I will give you rest. Take My yoke upon you, and learn of Me, for I am meek and lowly in heart, and you will find rest for your souls. For My yoke is easy, and My burden is light."

Matthew 11:28-30

Stress

You give power to the faint, and to those who have no might, You increase strength.

Isaiah 40:29

They cry to You, LORD, in their trouble, and You bring them out of their distresses. You make the storm calm so that the waves are still. Then they are glad because they [the waves] are quiet, so You bring them to their desired haven.

Psalm 107:28-30

Even the youths will faint and be weary, and the young men will utterly fall, but those who wait on You, LORD, shall renew their strength. They shall mount up with wings as eagles; they will run and not be weary, and they shall walk and not faint.

Isaiah 40:30-31

When I said, "My foot slips," Your mercy, O LORD, held me up. In the multitude of my thoughts within me, Your comforts delight my soul.

Psalm 94:18-19

STRESS

"Be still and know that I am God. I will be exalted
among the heathen; I will be exalted in the earth."
The LORD of hosts is with me; the God of Jacob is
my refuge.

Psalm 46:10-11

[Jesus] arose and rebuked the wind and said to the sea,
"Peace, be still." And the wind ceased, and there was a
great calm. And He said to them, "Why are you so
fearful? How is it that you have no faith?"
And they feared exceedingly and said to one another,
"What manner of man is this that even the wind and
the sea obey Him?"

Mark 4:39-41

Drop thy still dews of quietness,
Till all our strivings cease;
Take from our souls the strain and stress,
And let our ordered lives confess
The beauty of thy peace.

John Greenleaf Whittier

217

TEMPTATION

*Y*ou are able to keep me from falling and to present
me faultless before the presence of Your glory with
exceeding joy.

Jude 24

"I [God] give more grace. Which is why I say, 'I resist
the proud but give grace to the humble.' Submit
yourselves therefore to Me, your God. Resist the devil,
and he will flee from you."

James 4:6-7

You, Lord, know how to deliver the godly out
of temptations.

2 Peter 2:9

"Let the one who thinks he stands take heed lest he
fall. There is no temptation taken you but such as is
common to man. But I, your God, am faithful, who will
not allow you to be tempted above what you are able,
but will with the temptation also make a way to escape,
that you may be able to bear it."

1 Corinthians 10:12-13

Temptation

I am of You, God, and have overcome them [false
spirits and prophets], because greater is He that is in
me, than he that is in the world.

1 John 4:4

Sin shall not have dominion over me, for I am not
under the law but under grace.

Romans 6:14

"Count it all joy when you fall into various temptations,
knowing that the trying of your faith works patience.
But let patience have her perfect work, that you may be
perfect and entire, wanting nothing. . . . Blessed is the
one who endures temptation, for when he is tried, he
will receive the crown of life, which I, your Lord, have
promised to those who love Him."

James 1:2-4,12

"Do not be wise in your own eyes. Fear your LORD,
and depart from evil. It will be health to your navel and
nourishment to your bones."

Proverbs 3:7-8

Temptation

"You who love the LORD, hate evil. I preserve the souls of My saints; I deliver them out of the hand of the wicked."

Psalm 97:10

I do not have a high priest who cannot be touched with the feeling of my infirmities; but He was in all points tempted like I am, yet without sin. I, therefore, come boldly to the throne of grace, that I may obtain mercy and find grace to help in time of need.

Hebrews 4:15-16

God, You are my refuge and strength, a very present help in trouble.

Psalm 46:1

In that [Jesus] Himself has suffered being tempted, He is able to help those [like me] who are tempted.

Hebrews 2:18

"Keep your heart with all diligence, for out of it are the issues of life."

Proverbs 4:23

Your word have I hidden in my heart, that I might not sin against You. Blessed are You, O LORD.

Psalm 119:10-11

TEMPTATION

Have mercy on me, O God, according to Your lovingkindness. According to the multitude of Your tender mercies, blot out my transgressions. Wash me thoroughly from my offense, and cleanse me from my sin. For I acknowledge my transgressions, and my sin is ever before me. . . . Behold, You desire truth in the inward parts; and in the hidden part You will make me to know wisdom.

Psalm 51:1-3,6

Let no one say when he is tempted, I am tempted of God, for God cannot be tempted with evil, neither does He tempt anyone. But every person is tempted, when he is drawn away of his own lust and enticed.

James 1:13-14

My eyes are ever toward You, LORD; for You shall pluck my feet out of the net. . . . Let integrity and uprightness preserve me, for I wait on You.

Psalm 25:15,21

TEMPTATION

Who can understand his errors? LORD, cleanse me
from secret faults. Keep back Your servant also from
presumptuous sins; do not let them have dominion over
me. Then I will be upright, and I will be innocent from
the great transgression.

Psalm 19:12-13

When wisdom enters into my heart and knowledge is
pleasant to my soul, discretion will preserve me,
understanding will keep me, to deliver me from the way
of the evil man, from the one who speaks perverse
things, who leaves the paths of uprightness to walk in
the ways of darkness . . . to deliver me from the strange
woman, even from the stranger who flatters with her
words, who forsakes the guide of her youth and forgets
the covenant of her God.

Proverbs 2:10-13,16-17

*To attempt to resist temptation, abandon bad habits,
and control passion in our own strength, is like attempting
to check by a spider's thread the progress of a ship.*

Benjamin Waugh

WORRY

"*D*o not worry about anything, but in everything by prayer and supplication with thanksgiving let your requests be made known to Me, your God. And My peace, which passes all understanding, will keep your hearts and minds through Christ Jesus."

Philippians 4:6-7

Where no counsel is, the people fall; but in the multitude of counselors, there is safety.

Proverbs 11:14

I will hear what You, God the LORD, will speak, for You will speak peace to Your people and to Your saints. But do not let them turn to folly again.

Psalm 85:8

I will both lay myself down in peace and sleep, for You only, LORD, make me dwell in safety.

Psalm 4:8

"Be diligent to make your calling and election sure, for if you do these things, you will never fall."

2 Peter 1:10

WORRY

You have also given me the shield of Your salvation.
Your right hand has held me up, and Your gentleness
has made me great. You have enlarged my steps under
me, so that my feet did not slip.

Psalm 18:35-36

God, You are my salvation. I will trust and not be
afraid, for You, the LORD JEHOVAH, are my strength
and my song. You also are become my salvation.

Isaiah 12:2

God, You have not given me the spirit of fear but of
power, and of love, and of a sound mind.

2 Timothy 1:7

My child, do not let [wisdom and understanding]
depart from your eyes; keep sound wisdom and
discretion. . . . When you lie down, you will not be
afraid. Yes, you will lie down, and your sleep will
be sweet.

Proverbs 3:21,24

"Humble yourself . . . casting all your care on Me, for I
care for you."

1 Peter 5:6-7

WORRY

"Take no thought, saying, 'What will we eat?' Or, 'What will we drink?' Or, 'With what will we be clothed?' . . . for your heavenly Father knows that you have need of all these things. But seek first the kingdom of God and His righteousness, and all these things will be added to you."

Matthew 6:31-33

Blessed is the one who trusts in You, LORD, and whose hope You are. For he will be as a tree planted by the waters, and that spreads out her roots by the river, and shall not fear when heat comes, but her leaf will be green, and will not be full of care in the year of drought, neither shall cease from yielding fruit.

Jeremiah 17:7-8

Your word is a lamp to my feet and a light to my path.

Psalm 119:105

Quick is the succession of human events; the cares of today are seldom the cares of tomorrow; and when we lie down at night, we may safely say to most of our troubles, "You have done your worst, and we shall meet no more."

William Cowper

31 SCRIPTURE AFFIRMATIONS FOR A TRANSFORMED YOU

A bit of the Book in the morning,
To order my onward way.
A bit of the Book in the evening,
To hallow the end of the day.

Margaret Sangster

Do not be conformed to this world,
but be transformed by the renewing of your mind,
that you may prove what the will of God is,
that which is good and acceptable and perfect.

Romans 12:2 NASB

FOR YOUR DAY

DAY 1

God, You did not send Your Son into the world
to condemn me, but so that through Him I might
be saved.

John 3:17

DAY 2

God, it is You who works in me both to will and to do
of Your good pleasure.

Philippians 2:13

DAY 3

God, I know that all things work together for my
good because I love You and am called according to
Your purpose.

Romans 8:28

DAY 4

God, You have not given me the spirit of fear but of
power, of love, and of a sound mind.

2 Timothy 1:7

DAY 5

If I lack wisdom, God, let me ask You for it. You give
liberally to me, and You do not reprimand me for
asking. And it shall be given to me.

James 1:5

DAY 6

I sought You, LORD, and You heard me, and delivered me from all my fears.

Psalm 34:4

DAY 7

I do not fear for You are with me. I am not dismayed for You are my God. You will strengthen me; yes, You will help me; yes, You will uphold me with the right hand of Your righteousness.

Isaiah 41:10

DAY 8

If I confess my sins, You are faithful and just to forgive me of my sins and to cleanse me from all unrighteousness.

1 John 1:9

DAY 9

Bless the LORD, O my soul, and do not forget His benefits. He forgives all my offenses; He heals all my diseases.

Psalm 103:2-3

DAY 10

This is the confidence that I have in Christ: if I ask anything according to His will, He hears me; and if I know that He hears me, whatever I ask, I know that I have the petitions that I desire of Him.

1 John 5:14-15

DAY 11

Your divine power has given to me all things that
pertain to life and godliness.

2 Peter 1:3

DAY 12

Peace Jesus leaves with me, His peace He gives to me.
He does not give to me as the world gives. I do not let
my heart be troubled, nor do I let it be afraid.

John 14:27

DAY 13

I am confident of this very thing, that You who have
begun a good work in me will perform it until the day
of Jesus Christ.

Philippians 1:6

DAY 14

LORD, You are my light and my salvation. Whom shall
I fear? You are the strength of my life. Of whom shall I
be afraid?

Psalm 27:1

DAY 15

You will keep me in perfect peace whose mind is fixed
on You, because I trust in You.

Isaiah 26:3

DAY 16

LORD, You will show me the path of life. In Your presence is fullness of joy. At Your right hand there are pleasures forever.

Psalm 16:11

DAY 17

You are my God and You shall supply all my need according to Your riches in glory by Christ Jesus.

Philippians 4:19

DAY 18

Christ has redeemed me from the curse of the law, being made a curse for me, for it is written, "Cursed is everyone who hangs on a tree." He did this so that the blessing of Abraham might come on me through Jesus Christ, that I might receive the promise of the Spirit through faith.

Galatians 3:13-14

DAY 19

LORD, You are my Redeemer, the Holy One of Israel. You are the LORD my God who teaches me to profit and leads me by the way that I should go.

Isaiah 48:17

DAY 20

I cast all of my care upon You, God, for You care for me.

1 Peter 5:7

DAY 21

If I abide in Christ and His words abide in me, I shall ask whatever I wish, and it shall be done for me.

John 15:7

DAY 22

LORD, You have turned my mourning into dancing. You have put off my mourning clothes and surrounded me with gladness.

Psalm 30:11

DAY 23

I give and it will be given to me—good measure, pressed down, shaken together, and running over, will men give to me. For with the same measure that I use, it shall be measured to me as well.

Luke 6:38

DAY 24

God, I am Your workmanship, created in Christ Jesus for good works, which You have before ordained that I should walk in them.

Ephesians 2:10

DAY 25

God, You are able to do exceedingly abundantly above all that I ask or think, according to the power that works in me.

Ephesians 3:20

DAY 26

God, if You are for me, who can be against me?

Romans 8:31

DAY 27

Now there is no condemnation to me who is in Christ Jesus and who does not walk after the flesh but after the Spirit.

Romans 8:1

DAY 28

By grace I am saved through faith, and it is not of myself; it is Your gift, God.

Ephesians 2:8

DAY 29

I acknowledged my sin to You, and I have not hidden my offense. I said, I will confess my transgressions to the LORD; and You forgave the iniquity of my sin.

Psalm 32:5

DAY 30

Whatever things I desire, when I pray, I believe that I receive them and I shall have them.

Mark 11:24

DAY 31

Faithful are You who has called me; You also will do it.

1 Thessalonians 5:24

CLASSIC BIBLE PASSAGES FOR MEDITATION

It is by meditation that we ransack our deep and false hearts, find out our secret enemies, come to grips with them, expel them, and arm ourselves against their re-entrance. By meditation, we make use of all good means, fit ourselves for all good duties. By meditation, we see our weaknesses, obtain redress, prevent temptations, cheer up our loneliness, temper our occasions of delight, get more light unto our knowledge, add more heat to our affections, put more life into our devotions. It is only by meditation that we are able to be strangers upon the earth as we are commanded to be, and by this we are brought to a right estimation of all earthly things. Learn it if you can, neglect it if you so desire, but the one who does so shall never find joy, neither in God, nor in themselves.
Bishop Joseph Hall.

Do not let this Book of the Law depart from
your mouth; meditate on it day and night, so
that you may be careful to do everything written
in it. Then you will be prosperous and successful.

Joshua 1:8 NIV

THE TEN COMMANDMENTS

$\mathcal{T}$hen God spoke all these words:

"I am the LORD your God, who brought you out of the land of Egypt where you were slaves.

"You must not have any other gods except me.

"You must not make for yourselves an idol that looks like anything in the sky above or on the earth below or in the water below the land. You must not worship or serve any idol, because I, the LORD your God, am a jealous God. If you hate me, I will punish your children, and even your grandchildren and great-grandchildren. But I show kindness to thousands who love me and obey my commands.

"You must not use the name of the LORD your God thoughtlessly; the LORD will punish anyone who misuses his name.

The Ten Commandments

"Remember to keep the Sabbath holy. Work and get everything done during six days each week, but the seventh day is a day of rest to honor the LORD your God. On that day no one may do any work: not you, your son or daughter, your male or female slaves, your animals, or the foreigners living in your cities. The reason is that in six days the LORD made everything—the sky, the earth, the sea, and everything in them. On the seventh day he rested. So the LORD blessed the Sabbath day and made it holy.

"Honor your father and your mother so that you will live a long time in the land that the LORD your God is going to give you.

"You must not murder anyone.

"You must not be guilty of adultery.

"You must not steal.

"You must not tell lies about your neighbor.

"You must not want to take your neighbor's house. You must not want his wife or his male or female slaves, or his ox or his donkey, or anything that belongs to your neighbor."

Exodus 20:1-17 NCV

A LIFE OF BLESSING

*B*lessed is the man
who does not walk in the counsel of the wicked
or stand in the way of sinners
or sit in the seat of mockers.
But his delight is in the law of the LORD,
and on his law he meditates day and night.
He is like a tree planted by streams of water,
which yields its fruit in season
and whose leaf does not wither.
Whatever he does prospers.
Not so the wicked!
They are like chaff
that the wind blows away.
Therefore the wicked will not stand in the judgment,
nor sinners in the assembly of the righteous.
For the LORD watches over the way of the righteous,
but the way of the wicked will perish.

Psalm 1 NIV

PRAYER OF
REPENTANCE

God, be merciful to me
 because you are loving.
Because you are always ready to be merciful,
wipe out all my wrongs.
Wash away all my guilt
and make me clean again.
I know about my wrongs,
and I can't forget my sin.
You are the only one I have sinned against;
I have done what you say is wrong.
You are right when you speak
and fair when you judge.
I was brought into this world in sin.
In sin my mother gave birth to me.
You want me to be completely truthful,
so teach me wisdom.
Take away my sin, and I will be clean.
Wash me, and I will be whiter than snow.
Make me hear sounds of joy and gladness;
let the bones you crushed be happy again.
Turn your face from my sins
and wipe out all my guilt.

PRAYER OF REPENTANCE

Create in me a pure heart, God,
and make my spirit right again.
Do not send me away from you
or take your Holy Spirit away from me.
Give me back the joy of your salvation.
Keep me strong by giving me a willing spirit.
Then I will teach your ways to those who do wrong,
and sinners will turn back to you.
God, save me from the guilt of murder,
God of my salvation,
and I will sing about your goodness.
Lord, let me speak
so I may praise you.
You are not pleased by sacrifices, or I would give them.
You don't want burnt offerings.
The sacrifice God wants is a broken spirit.
God, you will not reject a heart that is broken
    and sorry for sin.

                                    Psalm 51:1-17 NCV

THE LORD IS YOUR PROTECTION

*H*e who dwells in the shelter of the Most High
Will abide in the shadow of the Almighty.
I will say to the LORD, "My refuge and my fortress,
My God, in whom I trust!"
For it is He who delivers you from the snare of
     the trapper
And from the deadly pestilence.
He will cover you with His pinions,
And under His wings you may seek refuge;
His faithfulness is a shield and bulwark.
You will not be afraid of the terror by night,
Or of the arrow that flies by day;
Of the pestilence that stalks in darkness,
Or of the destruction that lays waste at noon.
A thousand may fall at your side
And ten thousand at your right hand,
But it shall not approach you.
You will only look on with your eyes
And see the recompense of the wicked.

THE LORD IS YOUR PROTECTION

For you have made the LORD, my refuge,
Even the Most High, your dwelling place.
No evil will befall you,
Nor will any plague come near your tent.
For He will give His angels charge concerning you,
To guard you in all your ways.
They will bear you up in their hands,
That you do not strike your foot against a stone.
You will tread upon the lion and cobra,
The young lion and the serpent you will trample down.
"Because he has loved Me, therefore I will deliver him;
I will set him securely on high, because he has known
    My name.
"He will call upon Me, and I will answer him;
I will be with him in trouble;
I will rescue him and honor him.
"With a long life I will satisfy him
And let him see My salvation."

Psalm 91 NASB

243

THE LORD SEARCHES
AND KNOWS ME

O Lord, you have examined my heart and know everything about me. You know when I sit or stand. When far away you know my every thought. You chart the path ahead of me and tell me where to stop and rest. Every moment you know where I am. You know what I am going to say before I even say it. You both precede and follow me, and place your hand of blessing on my head.

This is too glorious, too wonderful to believe! I can *never* be lost to your Spirit! I can *never* get away from my God! If I go up to heaven, you are there; if I go down to the place of the dead, you are there. If I ride the morning winds to the farthest oceans, even there your hand will guide me, your strength will support me. If I try to hide in the darkness, the night becomes light around me. For even darkness cannot hide from God; to you the night shines as bright as day. Darkness and light are both alike to you.

THE LORD SEARCHES AND KNOWS ME

You made all the delicate, inner parts of my body and knit them together in my mother's womb. Thank you for making me so wonderfully complex! It is amazing to think about. Your workmanship is marvelous—and how well I know it. You were there while I was being formed in utter seclusion! You saw me before I was born and scheduled each day of my life before I began to breathe. Every day was recorded in your Book!

How precious it is, Lord, to realize that you are thinking about me constantly! I can't even count how many times a day your thoughts turn towards me. And when I waken in the morning, you are still thinking of me! . . .

Search me, O God, and know my heart; test my thoughts. Point out anything you find in me that makes you sad, and lead me along the path of everlasting life.

Psalm 139:1-18,23-24 TLB

GOD'S WAYS
ARE HIGHER

*H*o, everyone who thirsts,
come to the waters;
and you that have no money,
come, buy and eat!
Come, buy wine and milk
without money and without price.
Why do you spend your money for that which is
    not bread,
and your labor for that which does not satisfy?
Listen carefully to me, and eat what is good,
and delight yourselves in rich food.
Incline your ear, and come to me;
listen, so that you may live.
I will make with you an everlasting covenant,
my steadfast, sure love for David. . . .

Seek the LORD while he may be found,
call upon him while he is near;
let the wicked forsake their way,
and the unrighteous their thoughts;
let them return to the LORD, that he may have
    mercy on them,
and to our God, for he will abundantly pardon.

GOD'S WAYS ARE HIGHER

For my thoughts are not your thoughts,
nor are your ways my ways, says the LORD.
For as the heavens are higher than the earth,
so are my ways higher than your ways
and my thoughts than your thoughts.
For as the rain and the snow come down from heaven,
and do not return there until they have watered
    the earth,
making it bring forth and sprout,
giving seed to the sower and bread to the eater,
so shall my word be that goes out from my mouth;
it shall not return to me empty,
but it shall accomplish that which I purpose,
and succeed in the thing for which I sent it.
For you shall go out in joy,
and be led back in peace;
the mountains and the hills before you
shall burst into song,
and all the trees of the field shall clap their hands.

Isaiah 55:1-3,6-12 NRSV

THE BEATITUDES

*W*hen Jesus saw the crowds, He went up on the
mountain; and after He sat down, His disciples came
to Him. He opened His mouth and began to teach
them, saying,

"Blessed are the poor in spirit, for theirs is the kingdom
of heaven.
"Blessed are those who mourn, for they shall
be comforted.
"Blessed are the gentle, for they shall inherit the earth.
"Blessed are those who hunger and thirst for
righteousness, for they shall be satisfied.
"Blessed are the merciful, for they shall receive mercy.
"Blessed are the pure in heart, for they shall see God.
"Blessed are the peacemakers, for they shall be called
sons of God.
"Blessed are those who have been persecuted for the
sake of righteousness, for theirs is the kingdom
of heaven.
"Blessed are you when people insult you and persecute
you, and falsely say all kinds of evil against you
because of Me.
"Rejoice and be glad, for your reward in heaven is great;
for in the same way they persecuted the prophets
who were before you."

Matthew 5:1-12 NASB

LOVE YOUR ENEMIES

"You have heard that it was said, 'Love your neighbor and hate your enemy.' But I tell you: Love your enemies and pray for those who persecute you, that you may be sons of your Father in heaven. He causes his sun to rise on the evil and the good, and sends rain on the righteous and the unrighteous. If you love those who love you, what reward will you get? Are not even the tax collectors doing that? And if you greet only your brothers, what are you doing more than others? Do not even pagans do that? Be perfect, therefore, as your heavenly Father is perfect."

Matthew 5:43-48 NIV

THE LORD'S PRAYER

"In this manner, therefore, pray:

Our Father in heaven,
Hallowed be Your name.
Your kingdom come.
Your will be done
On earth as *it is* in heaven.
Give us this day our daily bread.
And forgive us our debts,
As we forgive our debtors.
And do not lead us into temptation,
But deliver us from the evil one.
For Yours is the kingdom and the power
and the glory forever. Amen.

"For if you forgive men their trespasses, your heavenly Father will also forgive you. But if you do not forgive men their trespasses, neither will your Father forgive your trespasses."

Matthew 6:9-15 NKJV

LOVE IS . . .

If I speak with human eloquence and angelic ecstasy but don't love, I'm nothing but the creaking of a rusty gate.

If I speak God's Word with power, revealing all his mysteries and making everything plain as day, and if I have faith that says to a mountain, "Jump," and it jumps, but I don't love, I'm nothing.

If I give everything I own to the poor and even go to the stake to be burned as a martyr, but I don't love, I've gotten nowhere. So, no matter what I say, what I believe, and what I do, I'm bankrupt without love.

Love never gives up.

Love cares more for others than for self.

LOVE IS . . .

> Love doesn't want what it doesn't have.
> Love doesn't strut,
> Doesn't have a swelled head,
> Doesn't force itself on others,
> Isn't always "me first,"
> Doesn't fly off the handle,
> Doesn't keep score of the sins of others,
> Doesn't revel when others grovel,
> Takes pleasure in the flowering of truth,
> Puts up with anything,
> Trusts God always,
> Always looks for the best,
> Never looks back,
> But keeps going to the end.

Love never dies. Inspired speech will be over some day; praying in tongues will end; understanding will reach its limit. We know only a portion of the truth, and what we say about God is always incomplete. But when the Complete arrives, our incompletes will be canceled.

LOVE IS . . .

When I was an infant at my mother's breast, I gurgled and cooed like any infant. When I grew up, I left those infant ways for good.

We don't yet see things clearly. We're squinting in a fog, peering through a mist. But it won't be long before the weather clears and the sun shines bright! We'll see it all then, see it all as clearly as God sees us, knowing him directly just as he knows us!

But for right now, until that completeness, we have three things to do to lead us toward that consummation: Trust steadily in God, hope unswervingly, love extravagantly. And the best of the three is love.

1 Corinthians 13 THE MESSAGE

You Will Know
Them by His Fruit

When the Holy Spirit controls our lives, he will produce this kind of fruit in us: love, joy, peace, patience, kindness, goodness, faithfulness, gentleness, and self-control. Here there is no conflict with the law.

Those who belong to Christ Jesus have nailed the passions and desires of their sinful nature to his cross and crucified them there. If we are living now by the Holy Spirit, let us follow the Holy Spirit's leading in every part of our lives.

Galatians 5:22-25 NLT

THE ARMOR OF GOD

$\mathcal{B}$e strong with the Lord's mighty power. Put on all of God's armor so that you will be able to stand firm against all strategies and tricks of the Devil. For we are not fighting against people made of flesh and blood, but against the evil rulers and authorities of the unseen world, against those mighty powers of darkness who rule this world, and against wicked spirits in the heavenly realms.

Use every piece of God's armor to resist the enemy in the time of evil, so that after the battle you will still be standing firm. Stand your ground, putting on the sturdy belt of truth and the body armor of God's righteousness. For shoes, put on the peace that comes from the Good News, so that you will be fully prepared. In every battle you will need faith as your shield to stop the fiery arrows aimed at you by Satan. Put on salvation as your helmet, and take the sword of the Spirit, which is the word of God. Pray at all times and on every occasion in the power of the Holy Spirit. Stay alert and be persistent in your prayers for all Christians everywhere.

Ephesians 6:10-18 NLT

INSTEAD OF WORRY, PRAY AND THINK ON THESE THINGS

Do not fret *or* have any anxiety about anything, but in every circumstance *and* in everything, by prayer and petition (definite requests), with thanksgiving, continue to make your wants known to God. And God's peace [shall be yours, that tranquil state of a soul assured of its salvation through Christ, and so fearing nothing from God and being content with its earthly lot of whatever sort that is, that peace] which transcends all understanding shall garrison *and* mount guard over your hearts and minds in Christ Jesus.

For the rest, brethren, whatever is true, whatever is worthy of reverence *and* is honorable *and* seemly, whatever is just, whatever is pure, whatever is lovely *and* lovable, whatever is kind *and* winsome *and* gracious, if there is any virtue *and* excellence, if there is anything worthy of praise, think on *and* weigh *and* take account of these things [fix your minds on them]. Practice what you have learned and received and heard and seen in me, *and* model your way of living on it, and the God of peace (of untroubled, undisturbed well-being) will be with you.

Philippians 4:6-9 AMP

FAITH IS . . .

$\mathcal{F}$aith means being sure of the things we hope for and knowing that something is real even if we do not see it. Faith is the reason we remember great people who lived in the past.

It is by faith we understand that the whole world was made by God's command so what we see was made by something that cannot be seen. . . .

Without faith no one can please God. Anyone who comes to God must believe that he is real and that he rewards those who truly want to find him.

Hebrews 11:1-3,6 NCV

WALKING IN
THE LIGHT

*T*his is the message we have heard from Him and announce to you, that God is Light, and in Him there is no darkness at all. If we say that we have fellowship with Him and yet walk in the darkness, we lie and do not practice the truth; but if we walk in the Light as He Himself is in the Light, we have fellowship with one another, and the blood of Jesus His Son cleanses us from all sin. If we say that we have no sin, we are deceiving ourselves and the truth is not in us. If we confess our sins, He is faithful and righteous to forgive us our sins and to cleanse us from all unrighteousness. If we say that we have not sinned, we make Him a liar and His word is not in us.

1 John 1:5-10 NASB

WORTHY IS THE LAMB

I saw in the right *hand* of Him who sat on the throne a scroll written inside and on the back, sealed with seven seals. Then I saw a strong angel proclaiming with a loud voice, "Who is worthy to open the scroll and to loose its seals?" And no one in heaven or on the earth or under the earth was able to open the scroll, or to look at it.

So I wept much, because no one was found worthy to open and read the scroll, or to look at it. But one of the elders said to me, "Do not weep. Behold, the Lion of the tribe of Judah, the Root of David, has prevailed to open the scroll and to loose its seven seals."

WORTHY IS THE LAMB

And I looked, and behold, in the midst of the throne and of the four living creatures, and in the midst of the elders, stood a Lamb as though it had been slain, having seven horns and seven eyes, which are the seven Spirits of God sent out into all the earth. Then He came and took the scroll out of the right hand of Him who sat on the throne.

Now when He had taken the scroll, the four living creatures and the twenty-four elders fell down before the Lamb, each having a harp, and golden bowls full of incense, which are the prayers of the saints. And they sang a new song, saying:

"You are worthy to take the scroll,
And to open its seals;
For You were slain,
And have redeemed us to God by Your blood
Out of every tribe and tongue and people and nation,
And have made us kings and priests to our God;
And we shall reign on the earth."

Revelation 5:1-10 NKJV

A NEW HEAVEN
AND A NEW EARTH

Now I saw a new heaven and a new earth, for the first heaven and the first earth had passed away. Also there was no more sea. Then I, John, saw the holy city, New Jerusalem, coming down out of heaven from God, prepared as a bride adorned for her husband. And I heard a loud voice from heaven saying, "Behold, the tabernacle of God *is* with men, and He will dwell with them, and they shall be His people. God Himself will be with them *and be* their God. And God will wipe away every tear from their eyes; there shall be no more death, nor sorrow, nor crying. There shall be no more pain, for the former things have passed away."

Revelation 21:1-4 NKJV

A loving Personality dominates the Bible, walking among the trees of the garden and breathing fragrance over every scene. Always a living Person is present, speaking, pleading, loving, working, and manifesting himself whenever and wherever his people have the receptivity necessary to receive the manifestation.

A.W. Tozer

STORIES OF GREAT CALLINGS AND GRADUATIONS IN THE BIBLE

*Every calling is great
when greatly pursued.*
Oliver Wendell Holmes

My brothers, be all the more eager to make your calling
and election sure. For if you do these things, you will
never fall, and you will receive a rich welcome into the
eternal kingdom of our Lord and Savior Jesus Christ.

2 Peter 1:10-11 NIV

GRADUATIONS IN THE BIBLE

DAVID

*T*he LORD said to Samuel, "How long will you grieve over Saul? I have rejected him from being king over Israel. Fill your horn with oil and set out; I will send you to Jesse the Bethlehemite, for I have provided for myself a king among his sons."

Samuel said, "How can I go? If Saul hears of it, he will kill me." And the LORD said, "Take a heifer with you, and say, 'I have come to sacrifice to the LORD.' Invite Jesse to the sacrifice, and I will show you what you shall do; and you shall anoint for me the one whom I name to you." Samuel did what the LORD commanded, and came to Bethlehem. The elders of the city came to meet him trembling, and said, "Do you come peaceably?" He said, "Peaceably; I have come to sacrifice to the LORD; sanctify yourselves and come with me to the sacrifice." And he sanctified Jesse and his sons and invited them to the sacrifice.

When they came, he looked on Eliab and thought, "Surely the LORD's anointed is now before the LORD." But the LORD said to Samuel, "Do not look on his appearance or on the height of his stature, because I have rejected him; for the LORD does not see as mortals see; they look on the outward appearance, but the LORD looks on the heart."

Then Jesse called Abinadab, and made him pass before Samuel. He said, "Neither has the LORD chosen this one." Then Jesse made Shammah pass by. And he said, "Neither has the LORD chosen this one." Jesse made seven of his sons pass before Samuel, and Samuel said to Jesse, "The LORD has not chosen any of these." Samuel said to Jesse, "Are all your sons here?" And he said, "There remains yet the youngest, but he is keeping the sheep." And Samuel said to Jesse, "Send and bring him; for we will not sit down until he comes here." He sent and brought him in. Now he was ruddy, and had beautiful eyes, and was handsome. The LORD said, "Rise and anoint him; for this is the one." Then Samuel took the horn of oil, and anointed him in the presence of his brothers; and the spirit of the LORD came mightily upon David from that day forward. Samuel then set out and went to Ramah.

1 Samuel 16:1-13 NRSV

GIDEON

*T*he angel of the LORD appeared to Gideon and said, "The LORD is with you, mighty warrior!"

Then Gideon said, "Sir, if the LORD is with us, why are we having so much trouble? Where are the miracles our ancestors told us he did when the LORD brought them out of Egypt? But now he has left us and has handed us over to the Midianites."

The LORD turned to Gideon and said, "Go with your strength and save Israel from the Midianites. I am the one who is sending you."

But Gideon answered, "Lord, how can I save Israel? My family group is the weakest in Manasseh, and I am the least important member of my family."

The LORD answered him, "I will be with you. It will seem as if the Midianites you are fighting are only one man."

. . . Then Gideon understood he had been talking to the angel of the LORD. So Gideon cried out, "Lord GOD! I have seen the angel of the LORD face to face!"

But the LORD said to Gideon, "Calm down! Don't be afraid! You will not die!"

So Gideon built an altar there to worship the LORD and named it The LORD Is Peace.

Judges 6:12-16,22-24 NCV

The Calling and Commission of Jeremiah

Now the word of the LORD came to me saying,
"Before I formed you in the womb I knew you,
And before you were born I consecrated you;
I have appointed you a prophet to the nations."
Then I said, "Alas, Lord GOD!
Behold, I do not know how to speak,
Because I am a youth."
But the LORD said to me,
"Do not say, 'I am a youth,'
Because everywhere I send you, you shall go,
And all that I command you, you shall speak.
"Do not be afraid of them,
For I am with you to deliver you," declares the LORD.
Then the LORD stretched out His hand and touched
my mouth, and the LORD said to me,
"Behold, I have put My words in your mouth.
"See, I have appointed you this day over the nations and
over the kingdoms,
To pluck up and to break down,
To destroy and to overthrow,
To build and to plant."

Jeremiah 1:4-10 NASB

Jesus' Calling Foretold

*F*or to us a child is born,
to us a son is given,
and the government will be on his shoulders.
And he will be called
Wonderful Counselor, Mighty God,
Everlasting Father, Prince of Peace.
Of the increase of his government and peace
there will be no end.
He will reign on David's throne
and over his kingdom,
establishing and upholding it
with justice and righteousness
from that time on and forever.

Isaiah 9:6-7 NIV

The Commissioning of Jesus

*W*hen He had been baptized, Jesus came up
immediately from the water; and behold, the heavens
were opened to Him, and He saw the Spirit of God
descending like a dove and alighting upon Him. And
suddenly a voice *came* from heaven, saying, "This is My
beloved Son, in whom I am well pleased."

Matthew 3:16-17 NKJV

JESUS WRESTLES WITH HIS CALL

$\mathcal{T}$hen Jesus went with his followers to a place called Gethsemane. He said to them, "Sit here while I go over there and pray." He took Peter and the two sons of Zebedee with him, and he began to be very sad and troubled. He said to them, "My heart is full of sorrow, to the point of death. Stay here and watch with me."

After walking a little farther away from them, Jesus fell to the ground and prayed, "My Father, if it is possible, do not give me this cup of suffering. But do what you want, not what I want."

Then Jesus went away a second time and prayed, "My Father, if it is not possible for this painful thing to be taken from me, and if I must do it, I pray that what you want will be done."

Then he went back to his followers, and again he found them asleep, because their eyes were heavy. So Jesus left them and went away and prayed a third time, saying the same thing.

Matthew 26:36-39,42-44 NCV

JESUS COMPLETES HIS MISSION

*T*hen Pilate laid open Jesus' back with a leaded whip, and the soldiers made a crown of thorns and placed it on his head and robed him in royal purple. "Hail, 'King of the Jews!'" they mocked, and struck him with their fists. . . .

And Pilate said to the Jews, "Here is your king!"

"Away with him," they yelled. "Away with him—crucify him!"

. . . Then Pilate gave Jesus to them to be crucified. So they had him at last, and he was taken out of the city, carrying his cross to the place known as "The Skull," in Hebrew, "Golgotha." There they crucified him. . . . And Pilate posted a sign over him reading, "Jesus of Nazareth, the King of the Jews."

Jesus knew that everything was now finished, and to fulfill the Scriptures said, "I'm thirsty." A jar of sour wine was sitting there, so a sponge was soaked in it and put on a hyssop branch and held up to his lips.

When Jesus had tasted it, he said, "It is finished," and bowed his head and dismissed his spirit.

John 19:1-3,14-19,28-30 KJV

271

. . . Jesus himself was suddenly standing there among them. He said, "Peace be with you. . . . "Yes, it was written long ago that the Messiah must suffer and die and rise again from the dead on the third day. With my authority, take this message of repentance to all the nations, beginning in Jerusalem: 'There is forgiveness of sins for all who turn to me.'

Luke 24:36,46-47 NLT

JOHN THE BAPTIST

John's Calling Foretold

Zacharias was in the sanctuary when suddenly an angel appeared, standing to the right of the altar of incense! Zacharias was startled and terrified. But the angel said, "Don't be afraid, Zacharias! For I have come to tell you that God has heard your prayer, and your wife Elizabeth will bear you a son! And you are to name him John. You will both have great joy and gladness at his birth, and many will rejoice with you. For he will be one of the Lord's great men. He must never touch wine or hard liquor—and he will be filled with the Holy Spirit, even from before his birth! And he will persuade many a Jew to turn to the Lord his God. He will be a man of rugged spirit and power like Elijah, the prophet of old; and he will precede the coming of the Messiah, preparing the people for his arrival. He will soften adult hearts to become like little children's, and will change disobedient minds to the wisdom of faith."

By now Elizabeth's waiting was over, for the time had come for the baby to be born—and it was a boy.

Then his father, Zacharias, was filled with the Holy Spirit and gave this prophecy:

"And you, my little son, shall be called the prophet of the glorious God, for you will prepare the way for the Messiah. You will tell his people how to find salvation through forgiveness of their sins. All this will be because the mercy of our God is very tender, and heaven's dawn is about to break upon us, to give light to those who sit in darkness and death's shadow, and to guide us to the path of peace."

The little boy greatly loved God and when he grew up he lived out in the lonely wilderness until he began his public ministry to Israel.

Luke 1:11-17,57,67,76-80 TLB

THE MINISTRY OF
JOHN THE BAPTIST

About that time John the Baptist began preaching in the desert area of Judea. John said, "Change your hearts and lives because the kingdom of heaven is near." John the Baptist is the one Isaiah the prophet was talking about when he said:

"This is a voice of one who calls out in the desert:
'Prepare the way for the Lord.
Make the road straight for him.'"

John's clothes were made from camel's hair, and he wore a leather belt around his waist. For food, he ate locusts and wild honey. Many people came from Jerusalem and Judea and all the area around the Jordan River to hear John. They confessed their sins, and he baptized them in the Jordan River.

Matthew 3:1-4 NCV

MARY

*I*n the sixth month of Elizabeth's pregnancy, God sent the angel Gabriel to Nazareth, a village in Galilee, to a virgin named Mary. She was engaged to be married to a man named Joseph, a descendant of King David. Gabriel appeared to her and said, "Greetings, favored woman! The Lord is with you!"

Confused and disturbed, Mary tried to think what the angel could mean. "Don't be frightened, Mary," the angel told her, "for God has decided to bless you! You will become pregnant and have a son, and you are to name him Jesus. He will be very great and will be called the Son of the Most High. And the Lord God will give him the throne of his ancestor David. And he will reign over Israel forever; his Kingdom will never end!"

Mary asked the angel, "But how can I have a baby? I am a virgin."

The angel replied, "The Holy Spirit will come upon you, and the power of the Most High will overshadow you. So the baby born to you will be holy, and he will be called the Son of God. . . . For nothing is impossible with God."

Mary responded, "I am the Lord's servant, and I am willing to accept whatever he wants. May everything you have said come true." And then the angel left.

Luke 1:26-35,37-38 NLT

275

MOSES

One day Moses was taking care of Jethro's flock. . . .
He came to Sinai, the mountain of God. There the
angel of the LORD appeared to him in flames of fire
coming out of a bush. Moses saw that the bush was on
fire, but it was not burning up. So he said, "I will go
closer to this strange thing. How can a bush continue
burning without burning up?"

When the LORD saw Moses was coming to look at the
bush, God called to him from the bush, "Moses,
Moses!"

And Moses said, "Here I am."

The LORD said, . . . "I have heard the cries of the
people of Israel, and I have seen the way the Egyptians
have made life hard for them. So now I am sending you
to the king of Egypt. Go! Bring my people, the
Israelites, out of Egypt!"

But Moses said to God, "I am not a great man! How
can I go to the king and lead the Israelites out of
Egypt?"

God said, "I will be with you. This will be the proof
that I am sending you: After you lead the people out of
Egypt, all of you will worship me on this mountain."

Moses said to God, "When I go to the Israelites, I will say to them, 'The God of your fathers sent me to you.' What if the people say, 'What is his name?' What should I tell them?"

Then God said to Moses, "I AM WHO I AM. When you go to the people of Israel, tell them, 'I AM sent me to you.'"

Then Moses answered, "What if the people of Israel do not believe me or listen to me? What if they say, 'The LORD did not appear to you'?"

The LORD said to him, "What is that in your hand?"

Moses answered, "It is my walking stick."

The LORD said, "Throw it on the ground."

So Moses threw it on the ground, and it became a snake. Moses ran from the snake, but the LORD said to him, "Reach out and grab the snake by its tail." When Moses reached out and took hold of the snake, it again became a stick in his hand. The LORD said, "This is so that the Israelites will believe that the LORD appeared to you. I am the God of their ancestors, the God of Abraham, the God of Isaac, and the God of Jacob."

But Moses said to the LORD, "Please, Lord, I have never been a skilled speaker. Even now, after talking to you, I cannot speak well. I speak slowly and can't find the best words."

Then the LORD said to him, "Who made a person's mouth? . . . It is I, the LORD. Now go! I will help you speak, and I will teach you what to say."

But Moses said, "Please, Lord, send someone else."

The LORD became angry with Moses and said, "Your brother Aaron, from the family of Levi, is a skilled speaker . . . You will speak to Aaron and tell him what to say. I will help both of you to speak and will teach you what to do. Aaron will speak to the people for you. You will tell him what God says, and he will speak for you. Take your walking stick with you, and use it to do the miracles."

So Moses took his wife and his sons, put them on a donkey, and started back to Egypt. He took with him the walking stick of God.

Exodus 3:1-4,7,9-14; 4:1-5,10-17,20 NCV

PAUL

*S*aul was still breathing out murderous threats against the Lord's disciples. . . . As he neared Damascus on his journey, suddenly a light from heaven flashed around him. He fell to the ground and heard a voice say to him, "Saul, Saul, why do you persecute me?"

"Who are you, Lord?" Saul asked.

"I am Jesus, whom you are persecuting," he replied. "Now get up and go into the city, and you will be told what you must do."

In Damascus there was a disciple named Ananias. The Lord called to him in a vision, "Ananias!"

"Yes, Lord," he answered.

The Lord told him, "Go to the house of Judas on Straight Street and ask for a man from Tarsus named Saul, for he is praying. In a vision he has seen a man named Ananias come and place his hands on him to restore his sight."

"Lord," Ananias answered, "I have heard many reports about this man and all the harm he has done to your saints in Jerusalem. And he has come here with authority from the chief priests to arrest all who call on your name."

But the Lord said to Ananias, "Go! This man is my chosen instrument to carry my name before the Gentiles and their kings and before the people of Israel. I will show him how much he must suffer for my name."

Then Ananias went to the house and entered it. Placing his hands on Saul, he said, "Brother Saul, the Lord—Jesus, who appeared to you on the road as you were coming here—has sent me so that you may see again and be filled with the Holy Spirit."

Immediately, something like scales fell from Saul's eyes, and he could see again. He got up and was baptized, and after taking some food, he regained his strength. Saul spent several days with the disciples in Damascus. At once he began to preach in the synagogues that Jesus is the Son of God.

Acts 9:1,3-6,10-20 NIV

PRAYERS OF THE BIBLE
FOR GRADUATES

*M*ake me what thou wouldst have
me; I bargain for nothing; I make no
terms; I seek for no previous information
whither thou art taking me; I will be
what thou wilt make me, and all that
thou wilt make me. I say not, I will
follow thee whithersoever thou goest,
for I am weak; but I give myself
to thee to lead me anywhere.

Cardinal John Henry Newman

The LORD bless you and keep you; the LORD make
his face shine upon you and be gracious to you; the
LORD turn his face toward you and give you peace.

Numbers 6:24-26 NIV

JESUS

$\mathcal{J}$esus spoke these things; and lifting up His eyes to heaven, He said, "Father, the hour has come; glorify Your Son, that the Son may glorify You, even as You gave Him authority over all flesh, that to all whom You have given Him, He may give eternal life. This is eternal life, that they may know You, the only true God, and Jesus Christ whom You have sent. I glorified You on the earth, having accomplished the work which You have given Me to do. Now, Father, glorify Me together with Yourself, with the glory which I had with You before the world was.

"I have manifested Your name to the men whom You gave Me out of the world; they were Yours and You gave them to Me, and they have kept Your word. Now they have come to know that everything You have given Me is from You; for the words which You gave Me I have given to them; and they received them and truly understood that I came forth from You, and they believed that You sent Me. I ask on their behalf; I do not ask on behalf of the world, but of those whom You have given Me; for they are Yours; and all things that are Mine are Yours, and Yours are Mine; and I have been glorified in them. I am no longer in the world; and yet they themselves are in the world, and I come to You. Holy Father, keep them in Your name, the name which

JESUS

You have given Me, that they may be one even as We are. While I was with them, I was keeping them in Your name which You have given Me; and I guarded them and not one of them perished but the son of perdition, so that the Scripture would be fulfilled.

"But now I come to You; and these things I speak in the world so that they may have My joy made full in themselves. I have given them Your word; and the world has hated them, because they are not of the world, even as I am not of the world. I do not ask You to take them out of the world, but to keep them from the evil one. They are not of the world, even as I am not of the world. Sanctify them in the truth; Your word is truth. As You sent Me into the world, I also have sent them into the world. For their sakes I sanctify Myself, that they themselves also may be sanctified in truth.

JESUS

"I do not ask on behalf of these alone, but for those also who believe in Me through their word; that they may all be one; even as You, Father, are in Me and I in You, that they also may be in Us, so that the world may believe that You sent Me.

"The glory which You have given Me I have given to them, that they may be one, just as We are one; I in them and You in Me, that they may be perfected in unity, so that the world may know that You sent Me, and loved them, even as You have loved Me. Father, I desire that they also, whom You have given Me, be with Me where I am, so that they may see My glory which You have given Me, for You loved Me before the foundation of the world.

"O righteous Father, although the world has not known You, yet I have known You; and these have known that You sent Me; and I have made Your name known to them, and will make it known, so that the love with which You loved Me may be in them, and I in them."

John 17:1-26 NASB

PAUL

After I heard of your faith in the Lord Jesus and your love for all the saints, do not cease to give thanks for you, making mention of you in my prayers: that the God of our Lord Jesus Christ, the Father of glory, may give to you the spirit of wisdom and revelation in the knowledge of Him, the eyes of your understanding being enlightened; that you may know what is the hope of His calling, what are the riches of the glory of His inheritance in the saints, and what *is* the exceeding greatness of His power toward us who believe, according to the working of His mighty power which He worked in Christ when He raised Him from the dead and seated *Him* at His right hand in the heavenly *places*.

Ephesians 1:15-20 NKJV

For this reason I bow my knees to the Father of our Lord Jesus Christ, from whom the whole family in heaven and earth is named, that He would grant you, according to the riches of His glory, to be strengthened with might through His Spirit in the inner man, that Christ may dwell in your hearts through faith; that you, being rooted and grounded in love, may be able to comprehend with all the saints what *is* the width and length and depth and height—to know the love of Christ which passes knowledge; that you may be filled with all the fullness of God.

PAUL

Now to Him who is able to do exceedingly abundantly
above all that we ask or think, according to the power
that works in us, to Him *be* glory in the church by
Christ Jesus to all generations, forever and ever. Amen.

Ephesians 3:14-21 NKJV

For this reason, since the day we heard about you, we
have not stopped praying for you and asking God to fill
you with the knowledge of his will through all spiritual
wisdom and understanding. And we pray this in order
that you may live a life worthy of the Lord and may
please him in every way: bearing fruit in every good
work, growing in the knowledge of God, being
strengthened with all power according to his glorious
might so that you may have great endurance and
patience, and joyfully giving thanks to the Father, who
has qualified you to share in the inheritance of the
saints in the kingdom of light.

Colossians 1:9-12 NIV

THROUGH THE BIBLE
IN ONE YEAR

A knowledge of the Bible without a
college course is more valuable than a
college course without the Bible.

Williams Lyon Phelps

There's nothing like the written Word of God for
showing you the way to salvation through faith in
Christ Jesus. Every part of Scripture is God-breathed
and useful one way or another—showing us truth,
exposing our rebellion, correcting our mistakes, training
us to live God's way. Through the Word we are put
together and shaped up for the tasks God has for us

2 Timothy 3:15-17 THE MESSAGE

IN ONE YEAR

January

1. Genesis 1-2; Psalm 1; Matthew 1-2
2. Genesis 3-4; Psalm 2; Matthew 3-4
3. Genesis 5-7; Psalm 3; Matthew 5
4. Genesis 8-9; Psalm 4; Matthew 6-7
5. Genesis 10-11; Psalm 5; Matthew 8-9
6. Genesis 12-13; Psalm 6; Matthew 10-11
7. Genesis 14-15; Psalm 7; Matthew 12
8. Genesis 16-17; Psalm 8; Matthew 13
9. Genesis 18-19; Psalm 9; Matthew 14-15
10. Genesis 20-21; Psalm 10; Matthew 16-17
11. Genesis 22-23; Psalm 11; Matthew 18
12. Genesis 24; Psalm 12; Matthew 19-20
13. Genesis 25-26; Psalm 13; Matthew 21
14. Genesis 27-28; Psalm 14; Matthew 22
15. Genesis 29-30; Psalm 15; Matthew 23
16. Genesis 31-32; Psalm 16; Matthew 24
17. Genesis 33-34; Psalm 17; Matthew 25
18. Genesis 35-36; Psalm 18; Matthew 26
19. Genesis 37-38; Psalm 19; Matthew 27
20. Genesis 39-40; Psalm 20; Matthew 28
21. Genesis 41-42; Psalm 21; Mark 1
22. Genesis 43-44; Psalm 22; Mark 2
23. Genesis 45-46; Psalm 23; Mark 3
24. Genesis 47-48; Psalm 24; Mark 4
25. Genesis 49-50; Psalm 25; Mark 5
26. Exodus 1-2; Psalm 26; Mark 6
27. Exodus 3-4; Psalm 27; Mark 7
28. Exodus 5-6; Psalm 28; Mark 8
29. Exodus 7-8; Psalm 29; Mark 9
30. Exodus 9-10; Psalm 30; Mark 10
31. Exodus 11-12; Psalm 31; Mark 11

February

1. Exodus 13-14; Psalm 32; Mark 12
2. Exodus 15-16; Psalm 33; Mark 13
3. Exodus 17-18; Psalm 34; Mark 14
4. Exodus 19-20; Psalm 35; Mark 15
5. Exodus 21-22; Psalm 36; Mark 16
6. Exodus 23-24; Psalm 37; Luke 1
7. Exodus 25-26; Psalm 38; Luke 2
8. Exodus 27-28; Psalm 39; Luke 3
9. Exodus 29-30; Psalm 40; Luke 4
10. Exodus 31-32; Psalm 41; Luke 5
11. Exodus 33-34; Psalm 42; Luke 6
12. Exodus 35-36; Psalm 43; Luke 7
13. Exodus 37-38; Psalm 44; Luke 8
14. Exodus 39-40; Psalm 45; Luke 9
15. Leviticus 1-2; Psalm 46; Luke 10
16. Leviticus 3-4; Psalm 47; Luke 11
17. Leviticus 5-6; Psalm 48; Luke 12
18. Leviticus 7-8; Psalm 49; Luke 13
19. Leviticus 9-10; Psalm 50; Luke 14
20. Leviticus 11-12; Psalm 51; Luke 15
21. Leviticus 13; Psalm 52; Luke 16
22. Leviticus 14; Psalm 53; Luke 17
23. Leviticus 15-16; Psalm 54; Luke 18
24. Leviticus 17-18; Psalm 55; Luke 19
25. Leviticus 19-20; Psalm 56; Luke 20
26. Leviticus 21-22; Psalm 57; Luke 21
27. Leviticus 23-24; Psalm 58; Luke 22
28. Leviticus 25; Psalm 59; Luke 23

March

1. Leviticus 26-27; Psalm 60; Luke 24
2. Numbers 1-2; Psalm 61; John 1
3. Numbers 3-4; Psalm 62; John 2-3
4. Numbers 5-6; Psalm 63; John 4
5. Numbers 7; Psalm 64; John 5
6. Numbers 8-9; Psalm 65; John 6
7. Numbers 10-11; Psalm 66; John 7
8. Numbers 12-13; Psalm 67; John 8
9. Numbers 14-15; Psalm 68; John 9
10. Numbers 16; Psalm 69; John 10
11. Numbers 17-18; Psalm 70; John 11
12. Numbers 19-20; Psalm 71; John 12
13. Numbers 21-22; Psalm 72; John 13
14. Numbers 23-24; Psalm 73; John 14-15
15. Numbers 25-26; Psalm 74; John 16
16. Numbers 27-28; Psalm 75; John 17
17. Numbers 29-30; Psalm 76; John 18
18. Numbers 31-32; Psalm 77; John 19
19. Numbers 33-34; Psalm 78; John 20
20. Numbers 35-36; Psalm 79; John 21
21. Deuteronomy 1-2; Psalm 80; Acts 1
22. Deuteronomy 3-4; Psalm 81; Acts 2
23. Deuteronomy 5-6; Psalm 82; Acts 3-4
24. Deuteronomy 7-8; Psalm 83; Acts 5-6
25. Deuteronomy 9-10; Psalm 84; Acts 7
26. Deuteronomy 11-12; Psalm 85; Acts 8
27. Deuteronomy 13-14; Psalm 86; Acts 9
28. Deuteronomy 15-16; Psalm 87; Acts 10
29. Deuteronomy 17-18; Psalm 88; Acts 11-12
30. Deuteronomy 19-20; Psalm 89; Acts 13
31. Deuteronomy 21-22; Psalm 90; Acts 14

April

1. Deuteronomy 23-24; Psalm 91; Acts 15
2. Deuteronomy 25-27; Psalm 92; Acts 16
3. Deuteronomy 28-29; Psalm 93; Acts 17
4. Deuteronomy 30-31; Psalm 94; Acts 18
5. Deuteronomy 32; Psalm 95; Acts 19
6. Deuteronomy 33-34; Psalm 96; Acts 20
7. Joshua 1-2; Psalm 97; Acts 21
8. Joshua 3-4; Psalm 98; Acts 22
9. Joshua 5-6; Psalm 99; Acts 23
10. Joshua 7-8; Psalm 100; Acts 24-25
11. Joshua 9-10; Psalm 101; Acts 26
12. Joshua 11-12; Psalm 102; Acts 27
13. Joshua 13-14; Psalm 103; Acts 28
14. Joshua 15-16; Psalm 104; Romans 1-2
15. Joshua 17-18; Psalm 105; Romans 3-4
16. Joshua 19-20; Psalm 106; Romans 5-6
17. Joshua 21-22; Psalm 107; Romans 7-8
18. Joshua 23-24; Psalm 108; Romans 9-10
19. Judges 1-2; Psalm 109; Romans 11-12
20. Judges 3-4; Psalm 110; Romans 13-14
21. Judges 5-6; Psalm 111; Romans 15-16
22. Judges 7-8; Psalm 112; 1 Corinthians 1-2
23. Judges 9; Psalm 113; 1 Corinthians 3-4
24. Judges 10-11; Psalm 114; 1 Corinthians 5-6
25. Judges 12-13; Psalm 115; 1 Corinthians 7
26. Judges 14-15; Psalm 116; 1 Corinthians 8-9
27. Judges 16-17; Psalm 117; 1 Corinthians 10
28. Judges 18-19; Psalm 118; 1 Corinthians 11
29. Judges 20-21; Psalm 119:1-88; 1 Corinthians 12
30. Ruth 1-4; Psalm 119:89-176; 1 Corinthians 13

May

1. 1 Samuel 1-2; Psalm 120; 1 Corinthians 14
2. 1 Samuel 3-4; Psalm 121; 1 Corinthians 15
3. 1 Samuel 5-6; Psalm 122; 1 Corinthians 16
4. 1 Samuel 7-8; Psalm 123; 2 Corinthians 1
5. 1 Samuel 9-10; Psalm 124; 2 Corinthians 2-3
6. 1 Samuel 11-12; Psalm 125; 2 Corinthians 4-5
7. 1 Samuel 13-14; Psalm 126; 2 Corinthians 6-7
8. 1 Samuel 15-16; Psalm 127; 2 Corinthians 8
9. 1 Samuel 17; Psalm 128; 2 Corinthians 9-10
10. 1 Samuel 18-19; Psalm 129; 2 Corinthians 11
11. 1 Samuel 20-21; Psalm 130; 2 Corinthians 12
12. 1 Samuel 22-23; Psalm 131; 2 Corinthians 13
13. 1 Samuel 24-25; Psalm 132; Galatians 1-2
14. 1 Samuel 26-27; Psalm 133; Galatians 3-4
15. 1 Samuel 28-29; Psalm 134; Galatians 5-6
16. 1 Samuel 30-31; Psalm 135; Ephesians 1-2
17. 2 Samuel 1-2; Psalm 136; Ephesians 3-4
18. 2 Samuel 3-4; Psalm 137; Ephesians 5-6
19. 2 Samuel 5-6; Psalm 138; Philippians 1-2
20. 2 Samuel 7-8; Psalm 139; Philippians 3-4
21. 2 Samuel 9-10; Psalm 140; Colossians 1-2
22. 2 Samuel 11-12; Psalm 141; Colossians 3-4
23. 2 Samuel 13-14; Psalm 142; 1 Thessalonians 1-2
24. 2 Samuel 15-16; Psalm 143; 1 Thessalonians 3-4
25. 2 Samuel 17-18; Psalm 144; 1 Thessalonians 5
26. 2 Samuel 19; Psalm 145; 2 Thessalonians 1-3
27. 2 Samuel 20-21; Psalm 146; 1 Timothy 1-2
28. 2 Samuel 22; Psalm 147; 1 Timothy 3-4
29. 2 Samuel 23-24; Psalm 148; 1 Timothy 5-6
30. 1 Kings 1; Psalm 149; 2 Timothy 1-2
31. 1 Kings 2-3; Psalm 150; 2 Timothy 3-4

June

1. 1 Kings 4-5; Proverbs 1; Titus 1-3
2. 1 Kings 6-7; Proverbs 2; Philemon
3. 1 Kings 8; Proverbs 3; Hebrew 1-2
4. 1 Kings 9-10; Proverbs 4; Hebrew 3-4
5. 1 Kings 11-12; Proverbs 5; Hebrews 5-6
6. 1 Kings 13-14; Proverbs 6; Hebrews 7-8
7. 1 Kings 15-16; Proverbs 7; Hebrews 9-10
8. 1 Kings 17-18; Proverbs 8; Hebrews 11
9. 1 Kings 19-20; Proverbs 9; Hebrews 12
10. 1 Kings 21-22; Proverbs 10; Hebrews 13
11. 2 Kings 1-2; Proverbs 11; James 1
12. 2 Kings 3-4; Proverbs 12; James 2-3
13. 2 Kings 5-6; Proverbs 13; James 4-5
14. 2 Kings 7-8; Proverbs 14; 1 Peter 1
15. 2 Kings 9-10; Proverbs 15; 1 Peter 2-3
16. 2 Kings 11-12; Proverbs 16; 1 Peter 4-5
17. 2 Kings 13-14; Proverbs 17; 2 Peter 1-3
18. 2 Kings 15-16; Proverbs 18; 1 John 1-2
19. 2 Kings 17; Proverbs 19; 1 John 3-4
20. 2 Kings 18-19; Proverbs 20; 1 John 5
21. 2 Kings 20-21; Proverbs 21; 2 John
22. 2 Kings 22-23; Proverbs 22; 3 John
23. 2 Kings 24-25; Proverbs 23; Jude
24. 1 Chronicles 1; Proverbs 24; Revelation 1-2
25. 1 Chronicles 2-3; Proverbs 25; Revelation 3-5
26. 1 Chronicles 4-5; Proverbs 26; Revelation 6-7
27. 1 Chronicles 6-7; Proverbs 27; Revelation 8-10
28. 1 Chronicles 8-9; Proverbs 28; Revelation 11-12
29. 1 Chronicles 10-11; Proverbs 29; Revelation 13-14
30. 1 Chronicles 12-13; Proverbs 30, Revelation 15-17

IN ONE YEAR

July

1. 1 Chronicles 14-15; Proverbs 31; Revelation 18-19
2. 1 Chronicles 16-17; Psalm 1; Revelation 20-22
3. 1 Chronicles 18-19; Psalm 2; Matthew 1-2
4. 1 Chronicles 20-21; Psalm 3; Matthew 3-4
5. 1 Chronicles 22-23; Psalm 4; Matthew 5
6. 1 Chronicles 24-25; Psalm 5; Matthew 6-7
7. 1 Chronicles 26-27; Psalm 6; Matthew 8-9
8. 1 Chronicles 28-29; Psalm 7; Matthew 10-11
9. 2 Chronicles 1-2; Psalm 8; Matthew 12
10. 2 Chronicles 3-4; Psalm 9; Matthew 13
11. 2 Chronicles 5-6; Psalm 10; Matthew 14-15
12. 2 Chronicles 7-8; Psalm 11; Matthew 16-17
13. 2 Chronicles 9-10; Psalm 12; Matthew 18
14. 2 Chronicles 11-12; Psalm 13; Matthew 19-20
15. 2 Chronicles 13-14; Psalm 14; Matthew 21
16. 2 Chronicles 15-16; Psalm 15; Matthew 22
17. 2 Chronicles 17-18; Psalm 16; Matthew 23
18. 2 Chronicles 19-20; Psalm 17; Matthew 24
19. 2 Chronicles 21-22; Psalm 18; Matthew 25
20. 2 Chronicles 23-24; Psalm 19; Matthew 26
21. 2 Chronicles 25-26; Psalm 20; Matthew 27
22. 2 Chronicles 27-28; Psalm 21; Matthew 28
23. 2 Chronicles 29-30; Psalm 22; Mark 1
24. 2 Chronicles 31-32; Psalm 23; Mark 2
25. 2 Chronicles 33-34; Psalm 24; Mark 3
26. 2 Chronicles 35-36; Psalm 25; Mark 4
27. Ezra 1-2; Psalm 26; Mark 5
28. Ezra 3-4; Psalm 27; Mark 6
29. Ezra 5-6; Psalm 28; Mark 7
30. Ezra 7-8; Psalm 29; Mark 8
31. Ezra 9-10; Psalm 30; Mark 9

IN ONE YEAR

August

1. Nehemiah 1-2; Psalm 31; Mark 10
2. Nehemiah 3-4; Psalm 32; Mark 11
3. Nehemiah 5-6; Psalm 33; Mark 12
4. Nehemiah 7; Psalm 34; Mark 13
5. Nehemiah 8-9; Psalm 35; Mark 14
6. Nehemiah 10-11; Psalm 36; Mark 15
7. Nehemiah 12-13; Psalm 37; Mark 16
8. Esther 1-2; Psalm 38; Luke 1
9. Esther 3-4; Psalm 39; Luke 2
10. Esther 5-6; Psalm 40; Luke 3
11. Esther 7-8; Psalm 41; Luke 4
12. Esther 9-10; Psalm 42; Luke 5
13. Job 1-2; Psalm 43; Luke 6
14. Job 3-4; Psalm 44; Luke 7
15. Job 5-6; Psalm 45; Luke 8
16. Job 7-8; Psalm 46; Luke 9
17. Job 9-10; Psalm 47; Luke 10
18. Job 11-12; Psalm 48; Luke 11
19. Job 13-14; Psalm 49; Luke 12
20. Job 15-16; Psalm 50; Luke 13
21. Job 17-18; Psalm 51; Luke 14
22. Job 19-20; Psalm 52; Luke 15
23. Job 21-22; Psalm 53; Luke 16
24. Job 23-25; Psalm 54; Luke 17
25. Job 26-28; Psalm 55; Luke 18
26. Job 29-30; Psalm 56; Luke 19
27. Job 31-32; Psalm 57; Luke 20
28. Job 33-34; Psalm 58; Luke 21
29. Job 35-36; Psalm 59; Luke 22
30. Job 37-38; Psalm 60; Luke 23
31. Job 39-40; Psalm 61; Luke 24

September

1. Job 41-42; Psalm 62; John 1
2. Ecclesiastes 1-2; Psalm 63; John 2-3
3. Ecclesiastes 3-4; Psalm 64; John 4
4. Ecclesiastes 5-6; Psalm 65; John 5
5. Ecclesiastes 7-8; Psalm 66; John 6
6. Ecclesiastes 9-10; Psalm 67; John 7
7. Ecclesiastes 11-12; Psalm 68; John 8
8. Song of Solomon 1-2; Psalm 69; John 9
9. Song of Solomon 3-4; Psalm 70; John 10
10. Song of Solomon 5-6; Psalm 71; John 11
11. Song of Solomon 7-8; Psalm 72; John 12
12. Isaiah 1-2; Psalm 73; John 13
13. Isaiah 3-5; Psalm 74; John 14-15
14. Isaiah 6-8; Psalm 75; John 16
15. Isaiah 9-10; Psalm 76; John 17
16. Isaiah 11-13; Psalm 77; John 18
17. Isaiah 14-15; Psalm 78; John 19
18. Isaiah 16-17; Psalm 79; John 20
19. Isaiah 18-19; Psalm 80; John 21
20. Isaiah 20-22; Psalm 81; Acts 1
21. Isaiah 23-24; Psalm 82; Acts 2
22. Isaiah 25-26; Psalm 83; Acts 3-4
23. Isaiah 27-28; Psalm 84; Acts 5-6
24. Isaiah 29-30; Psalm 85; Acts 7
25. Isaiah 31-32; Psalm 86; Acts 8
26. Isaiah 33-34; Psalm 87; Acts 9
27. Isaiah 35-36; Psalm 88; Acts 10
28. Isaiah 37-38; Psalm 89; Acts 11-12
29. Isaiah 39-40; Psalm 90; Acts 13
30. Isaiah 41-42; Psalm 91; Acts 14

IN ONE YEAR

October

1. Isaiah 43-44; Psalm 92; Acts 15
2. Isaiah 45-46; Psalm 93; Acts 16
3. Isaiah 47-48; Psalm 94; Acts 17
4. Isaiah 49-50; Psalm 95; Acts 18
5. Isaiah 51-52; Psalm 96; Acts 19
6. Isaiah 53-54; Psalm 97; Acts 20
7. Isaiah 55-56; Psalm 98; Acts 21
8. Isaiah 57-58; Psalm 99; Acts 22
9. Isaiah 59-60; Psalm 100; Acts 23
10. Isaiah 61-62; Psalm 101; Acts 24-25
11. Isaiah 63-64; Psalm 102; Acts 26
12. Isaiah 65-66; Psalm 103; Acts 27
13. Jeremiah 1-2; Psalm 104; Acts 28
14. Jeremiah 3-4; Psalm 105; Romans 1-2
15. Jeremiah 5-6; Psalm 106; Romans 3-4
16. Jeremiah 7-8; Psalm 107; Romans 5-6
17. Jeremiah 9-10; Psalm 108; Romans 7-8
18. Jeremiah 11-12; Psalm 109; Romans 9-10
19. Jeremiah 13-14; Psalm 110; Romans 11-12
20. Jeremiah 15-16; Psalm 111; Romans 13-14
21. Jeremiah 17-18; Psalm 112; Romans 15-16
22. Jeremiah 19-20; Psalm 113; 1 Corinthians 1-2
23. Jeremiah 21-22; Psalm 114; 1 Corinthians 3-4
24. Jeremiah 23-24; Psalm 115; 1 Corinthians 5-6
25. Jeremiah 25-26; Psalm 116; 1 Corinthians 7
26. Jeremiah 27-28; Psalm 117; 1 Corinthians 8-9
27. Jeremiah 29-30; Psalm 118; 1 Corinthians 10
28. Jeremiah 31-32; Psalm 119: 1-64; 1 Corinthians 11
29. Jeremiah 33-34; Psalm 119:65-120; 1 Corinthians 12
30. Jeremiah 35-36; Psalm 119:121-176; 1 Corinthians 13
31. Jeremiah 37-38; Psalm 120; 1 Corinthians 14

IN ONE YEAR

November

1. Jeremiah 39-40; Psalm 121; 1 Corinthians 15
2. Jeremiah 41-42; Psalm 122; 1 Corinthians 16
3. Jeremiah 43-44; Psalm 123; 2 Corinthians 1
4. Jeremiah 45-46; Psalm 124; 2 Corinthians 2-3
5. Jeremiah 47-48; Psalm 125; 2 Corinthians 4-5
6. Jeremiah 49-50; Psalm 126; 2 Corinthians 6-7
7. Jeremiah 51-52; Psalm 127; 2 Corinthians 8
8. Lamentations 1-2; Psalm 128; 2 Corinthians 9-10
9. Lamentations 3; Psalm 129; 2 Corinthians 11
10. Lamentations 4-5; Psalm 130; 2 Corinthians 12
11. Ezekiel 1-2; Psalm 131; 2 Corinthians 13
12. Ezekiel 3-4; Psalm 132; Galatians 1-2
13. Ezekiel 5-6; Psalm 133; Galatians 3-4
14. Ezekiel 7-8; Psalm 134; Galatians 5-6
15. Ezekiel 9-10; Psalm 135; Ephesians 1-2
16. Ezekiel 11-12; Psalm 136; Ephesians 3-4
17. Ezekiel 13-14; Psalm 137; Ephesians 5-6
18. Ezekiel 15-16; Psalm 138; Philippians 1-2
19. Ezekiel 17-18; Psalm 139; Philippians 3-4
20. Ezekiel 19-20; Psalm 140; Colossians 1-2
21. Ezekiel 21-22; Psalm 141; Colossians 3-4
22. Ezekiel 23-24; Psalm 142; 1 Thessalonians 1-2
23. Ezekiel 25-26; Psalm 143; 1 Thessalonians 3-4
24. Ezekiel 27-28; Psalm 144; 1 Thessalonians 5
25. Ezekiel 29-30; Psalm 145; 2 Thessalonians 1-3
26. Ezekiel 31-32; Psalm 146; 1 Timothy 1-2
27. Ezekiel 33-34; Psalm 147; 1 Timothy 3-4
28. Ezekiel 35-36; Psalm 148; 1 Timothy 5-6
29. Ezekiel 37-38; Psalm 149; 2 Timothy 1-2
30. Ezekiel 39-40; Psalm 150; 2 Timothy 3-4

IN ONE YEAR

December

1. Ezekiel 41-42; Proverbs 1; Titus 1-3
2. Ezekiel 43-44; Proverbs 2; Philemon
3. Ezekiel 45-46; Proverbs 3; Hebrews 1-2
4. Ezekiel 47-48; Proverbs 4; Hebrews 3-4
5. Daniel 1-2; Proverbs 5; Hebrews 5-6
6. Daniel 3-4; Proverbs 6; Hebrews 7-8
7. Daniel 5-6; Proverbs 7; Hebrews 9-10
8. Daniel 7-8; Proverbs 8; Hebrews 11
9. Daniel 9-10; Proverbs 9; Hebrews 12
10. Daniel 11-12; Proverbs 10; Hebrews 13
11. Hosea 1-3; Proverbs 11; James 1-3
12. Hosea 4-6; Proverbs 12; James 4-5
13. Hosea 7-8; Proverbs 13; 1 Peter 1
14. Hosea 9-11; Proverbs 14; 1 Peter 2-3
15. Hosea 12-14; Proverbs 15; 1 Peter 4-5
16. Joel 1-3; Proverbs 16; 2 Peter 1-3
17. Amos 1-3; Proverbs 17; 1 John 1-2
18. Amos 4-6; Proverbs 18; 1 John 3-4
19. Amos 7-9; Proverbs 19; 1 John 5
20. Obadiah; Proverbs 20; 2 John
21. Jonah 1-4; Proverbs 21; 3 John
22. Micah 1-4; Proverbs 22; Jude
23. Micah 5-7; Proverbs 23; Revelation 1-2
24. Nahum 1-3; Proverbs 24; Revelation 3-5
25. Habakkuk 1-3; Proverbs 25; Revelation 6-7
26. Zephaniah 1-3; Proverbs 26; Revelation 8-10
27. Haggai 1-2; Proverbs 27; Revelation 11-12
28. Zechariah 1-4; Proverbs 28; Revelation 13-14
29. Zechariah 5-9; Proverbs 29; Revelation 15-17
30. Zechariah 10-14; Proverbs 30; Revelation 18-19
31. Malachi 1-4; Proverbs 31; Revelation 20-22

IN PRAISE OF
THE OVERCOMER

*I*n education everything is built up on
difficulty, there is always something to
overcome. And this is true in the spiritual
world. If the world, the flesh, and the
devil have knocked you out once, get up
and face them again, and again, until you
have done with them. That is how
character is made in the spiritual
domain as well as in the natural.

Oswald Chambers

"I have told you all this so that you will have
peace of heart and mind. Here on earth you
will have many trials and sorrows; but
cheer up, for I have overcome the world."

John 16:33 TLB

JOSHUA AND CALEB—
OLD TESTAMENT OVERCOMERS

*C*aleb quieted the people before Moses, and said, "Let us go up at once and take possession, for we are well able to overcome it."

But the men who had gone up with him said, "We are not able to go up against the people, for they *are* stronger than we." And they gave the children of Israel a bad report of the land which they had spied out, saying, "The land through which we have gone as spies *is* a land that devours its inhabitants, and all the people whom we saw in it *are* men of *great* stature. There we saw the giants . . . and we were like grasshoppers in our own sight, and so we were in their sight."

"Because all these men who have seen My glory and the signs which I did in Egypt and in the wilderness, and have put Me to the test now these ten times, and have not heeded My voice, they certainly shall not see the land of which I swore to their fathers, nor shall any of those who rejected Me see it. But My servant Caleb, because he has a different spirit in him and has followed Me fully, I will bring into the land where he went, and his descendants shall inherit it."

Numbers 13:30-33; 14:22-24 NKJV

OVERCOMING SAINTS

I write to you, fathers,
because you have known him who is from
    the beginning.
I write to you, young men,
because you have overcome the evil one.
I write to you, dear children,
because you have known the Father.
I write to you, fathers,
because you have known him who is from the beginning.
I write to you, young men,
because you are strong,
and the word of God lives in you,
and you have overcome the evil one.

1 John 2:13-14 NIV

You are of God, little children, and have overcome
them, because He who is in you is greater than he who
is in the world.

1 John 4:4 NKJV

Whatever is born of God overcomes the world. And
this is the victory that has overcome the world—our
faith. Who is he who overcomes the world, but he who
believes that Jesus is the Son of God?

1 John 5:4-5 NKJV

OVERCOMING SAINTS

"HE WHO HAS AN EAR, LET HIM HEAR WHAT THE SPIRIT SAYS TO THE CHURCHES."

"To him who overcomes . . .

*   I will give to eat from the tree of life, which is in the midst of the Paradise of God."

Revelation 2:7 NKJV

*   I will give some of the hidden manna to eat. And I will give him a white stone, and on the stone a new name written which no one knows except him who receives *it*."

Revelation 2:17 NKJV

*   I will grant to sit with Me on My throne, as I also overcame and sat down with My Father on His throne."

Revelation 3:21 NKJV

Overcoming Saints

"He who overcomes . . .
- shall not be hurt by the second death."

Revelation 2:11 NKJV

- and keeps My works until the end, to him I will give power over the nations."

Revelation 2:26 NKJV

- shall be clothed in white garments, and I will not blot out his name from the Book of Life; but I will confess his name before My Father and before His angels."

Revelation 3:5 NKJV

- I will make him a pillar in the temple of My God, and he shall go out no more. I will write on him the name of My God and the name of the city of My God, the New Jerusalem, which comes down out of heaven from My God. And *I will write on him* My new name."

Revelation 3:12 NKJV

- shall inherit all things, and I will be his God and he shall be My son."

Revelation 21:7 NKJV

THE LAMB—
THE ULTIMATE OVERCOMER

Now I saw heaven opened, and behold, a white horse. And He who sat on him *was* called Faithful and True, and in righteousness He judges and makes war. His eyes *were* like a flame of fire, and on His head *were* many crowns. He had a name written that no one knew except Himself. He *was* clothed with a robe dipped in blood, and His name is called The Word of God. And the armies in heaven, clothed in fine linen, white and clean, followed Him on white horses. Now out of His mouth goes a sharp sword, that with it He should strike the nations. And He Himself will rule them with a rod of iron. He Himself treads the winepress of the fierceness and wrath of Almighty God. And He has on *His* robe and on His thigh a name written:

KING OF KING AND LORD OF LORDS.

Revelation 19:11-16 NKJV

THE FINAL
MESSAGE

"*B*ehold, I am coming quickly, and My reward is with Me, to render to every man according to what he has done.

"I am the Alpha and the Omega, the first and the last, the beginning and the end."

Blessed are those who wash their robes, so that they may have the right to the tree of life, and may enter by the gates into the city. . . .

The Spirit and the bride say, "Come." And let the one who hears say, "Come." And let the one who is thirsty come; let the one who wishes take the water of life without cost.

I testify to everyone who hears the words of the prophecy of this book: if anyone adds to them, God will add to him the plagues which are written in this book; and if anyone takes away from the words of the book of this prophecy, God will take away his part from the tree of life and from the holy city, which are written in this book.

He who testifies to these things says, "Yes, I am coming quickly." Amen. Come, Lord Jesus.

The grace of the Lord Jesus be with all. Amen.

Revelation 22:12-14,17-21 NASB

A GRADUATE'S ANSWERS
TO PRAYERS

A prayer in its simplest definition is
merely a wish turned Godward.

Phillips Brooks

Don't worry about anything; instead, pray about
everything. Tell God what you need, and thank him for
all he has done. If you do this, you will experience
God's peace, which is far more wonderful than the
human mind can understand. His peace will guard
your hearts and minds as you live in Christ Jesus.

Philippians 4:6-7 NLT

PRAYERS AND ANSWERS

_____

_____

_____

_____

_____

_____

_____

_____

_____

_____

_____

_____

_____

_____

_____

_____

_____

_____

PRAYERS AND ANSWERS

_____

_____

_____

_____

_____

_____

_____

_____

_____

_____

_____

_____

_____

_____

PRAYERS AND ANSWERS

_____

_____

_____

_____

_____

_____

_____

_____

_____

_____

_____

_____

_____

_____

_____

Prayers and Answers

_____

_____

_____

_____

_____

_____

_____

_____

_____

_____

_____

_____

_____

_____

_____

_____

Prayers and Answers

Prayers and Answers

_____

_____

_____

_____

_____

_____

_____

_____

_____

_____

_____

_____

_____

_____

_____

_____

_____

REFERENCES

Additional copies of this book
are available from your local bookstore.

Also available:

My Personal Promise Bible for Teens
My Personal Promise Bible for Women
My Personal Promise Bible for Mothers

If you have enjoyed this book,
or if it has impacted your life,
we would like to hear from you.

Please contact us at:

Honor Books
Department E
P.O. Box 55388
Tulsa, Oklahoma 74155
Or by e-mail at *info@honorbooks.com*